Ministry
ᵒʳApostolate?

Ministry
or Apostolate?

What Should
the Catholic
Laity Be Doing?

Russell Shaw

Our Sunday Visitor Publishing Division
Our Sunday Visitor, Inc.
Huntington, Indiana 46750

Our Sunday Visitor Publishing Division
Our Sunday Visitor, Inc.
200 Noll Plaza
Huntington, IN 46750

ISBN: 0-87973-957-6
LCCCN: 2001135261

Cover design by Rebecca Heaston
Interior design by Sherri L. Hoffman

PRINTED IN THE UNITED STATES OF AMERICA

CONTENTS

ACKNOWLEDGMENTS

As on other occasions, I wish to express sincere thanks to Dr. Germain Grisez for his numerous helpful comments on the first draft of this book.

I also am grateful to Dr. Daniel Cere for having read and commented on the manuscript. The results, needless to say, are the author's responsibility, not theirs.

ONE

What Is the Problem?

Lay ministry or lay apostolate? If you put the question like that, the answer obviously is: *Both*. Both lay ministry (carried on in parishes and other ecclesiastical settings) and lay apostolate (carried out in the world) are admirable ways for Catholic laypeople to participate in the Church's mission. The Church is well served by both. Nothing that follows in this book should be understood as saying anything else.

But life is more complicated than just saying "Both" might seem to imply. Whether the problem lies in a human incapacity for holding two ideas in the mind at the same time or whether it lies somewhere else, it not uncommonly happens that one good thing is emphasized at the expense of another. That has happened in this case. During the last several decades, lay ministry has been emphasized in American Catholicism *at the expense of* lay apostolate. The result has been a serious setback to the Church's mission in the secular world.

A little later, I shall say more about what these two terms, "lay ministry" and "lay apostolate," signify here. For now, it will be enough to say that "ministry" is something people do within the framework of the Church and on its behalf — it is building up the Body of Christ, service rendered to the People of God themselves. And as such, it is very good. Forms of lay ministry like lector, cantor, and minister of the Eucharist are familiar to every churchgoing Catholic today.

"Apostolate," by contrast, is something done *outside* the confines of the Church — it is service rendered to the world and its people; it is evangelization, especially perhaps what these days is called the evangelization of culture. It is harder to say what an "apostle" looks like, because apostolate can take so many forms. Generally speaking, though, a lay apostle is someone consciously striving to meet her or his secular responsibilities — job, family, social life, commitments and relationships of all sorts — in a way that represents the living-out of the Gospel in ordinary life. Lay apostolate, too, is very good. (We shall get back to these definitions later.)

The problem is this. Starting in the late 1950s and continuing up to now, the apostolate of the laity — the effort to carry Christ's message into the highways and byways where people live and work — was seriously neglected. During roughly the same period, increasing and, in the circumstances, disproportionate attention was lavished on lay ministries — various functions and services performed by laypeople in religious institutions or on behalf of the Church. In particular, an unwarranted quantity of attention went to the numerically minuscule, elite form called Lay Ecclesial Ministry. (More about this later.)

This was a bad mistake. Not alone certainly, but in combination with a raft of other religious and social factors, the failure to motivate and form the Catholic people for lay apostolate helped erode both their will and their ability to respond to what the Second Vatican Council (1962-1965) called in its "Dogmatic Constitution on the Church" the laity's "special vocation," namely, "to make the Church present and fruitful in those places and circumstances where it is only through them that she can become the salt of the earth" (*Lumen Gentium*, 33).

A great deal of this book will be devoted to spelling out and documenting what has just been said. In the last chapter, I shall offer some suggestions about what must be done to change things for the better. I mean to keep what I say brief and to the point. But having begun by stressing the negative, let me continue stressing it for a while in order to make clear just how serious this problem really is.

A Weekend in Annapolis

In June of the millennium year 2000, I attended a conference organized by a couple of think tanks to discuss the role played by Catholics in American public life. The theme was "Patterns of Catholic Civic Engagement." The three dozen or so participants were the usual mix on such occasions: college professors, writers and journalists, and the like. Meeting in the lovely old city of Annapolis, Maryland, in a historic inn a few blocks from the U.S. Naval Academy, we spent a weekend reflecting on whether and how Catholics were making a distinctively *Catholic* contribution to society.

I had been invited to present a short paper at midpoint in the program as part of a panel on "Catholic Presence After Vatican II." I thought that in considering the question of "public presence" it would make sense to begin with how Catholics come across to everybody else — not how we like to think of ourselves, in other words, but how others think about us. Here is what I said:

"According to the Center for Media and Public Affairs, the quantity of Catholic coverage in national outlets like *The New York Times*, *The Washington Post*, the newsweeklies, and the evening news fell 50% from the 1960s through the 1990s. [The Center for Media and Public Affairs is an independent, nonpartisan organization in Washington, D.C., specializing in analysis of the news media. In recent years, it has conducted two large studies of how major U.S. secular news organizations covered the Catholic Church from the mid-1960s through the late 1990s.] There is nothing surprising about that, since Vatican II, the birth control controversy, and other Catholic excitements generated an abnormally large volume of coverage during the '60s. The drop-off was predictable.

"Something else was not. The Center for Media and Public Affairs also reports that the two big Catholic stories of the 1990s in the national media were clergy sex abuse and women's issues, including the controversy over ordination.

"The news judgment here was eminently sound. These really *were* the big Catholic stories of the decade. They even constituted public presence of a sort. But this was hardly a positive civic presence. It was the presence of a religious body wrestling publicly with its own urgent problems.

"Of course, someone might object that analyzing media coverage tells us about the public presence of the institutional Church but only about that. During this same period, the 1960s until now, haven't Catholics acting outside the institutional, ecclesiastical framework been the Catholic presence that counts?

"In general, and granting the exceptions, I think not. Since the 1960s — in fact, beginning two decades earlier — the American Catholic experience has been one of cultural assimilation, not the evangelization of culture. Catholics have been present to the culture by becoming part of it. That is not an entirely bad thing. But it has had a price, measured in the capacity to make a distinctive contribution to shaping the culture.

"Charles Morris remarks that the present challenge for the Church is very much like the challenge in the nineteenth century: 'how to create a Church that is both *American* and

Catholic, drawing from the best in both traditions.' The original solution, pursued with considerable success until the middle years of the twentieth century, was to create a largely self-contained Catholic subculture. Now the subculture has broken down, and the Church must grope to find a new arrangement. This process, as Morris says, is 'painful, public, and not very pretty; and it is still far from assured of success.' [Charles R. Morris, *American Catholic*. New York: Random House, 1997, pp. 411-412.]

"I recall the intellectuals' lament at my Catholic university in the 1950s: 'Where are the Catholic Salks? Where are the Catholic Einsteins?' Today it would be more to the point to ask: 'Where are the Catholic Dorothy Days, Fulton Sheens, Thomas Mertons, Flannery O'Connors, and John Courtney Murrays?' In other words: where are the *Catholic* Catholics?

"Back in April *The New York Times Magazine* published results of a poll on 'The Inner Life of Americans' along with commentaries. The findings confirm what other polls have found. Americans think people are born inherently good; two-thirds are pleased that their lives turned out as they did; they divide evenly on whether adulterous fantasies are wrong; 60% hold that it is sometimes necessary to lie (68% of the Catholics think it is). And so forth.

"The picture that emerges is of people who are optimistic and elastic. And something more. As Alan Wolfe remarks in one of the commentaries, 'Americans tend to be cynical about politicians, distrustful of institutions and civically disengaged. . . . In America, it is not the issue that matters. It is whether the issue is viewed as public or private. The public is what you have to do; the private is what you want to do.'

"Optimism, elasticity, and a strong preference for the private over the public are good enough things up to a point, but one would hesitate to fashion them into a philosophy of life. That, nevertheless, is what many Americans apparently have done, including many Catholics.

"There is virtually no difference between Catholics and Protestants in this *Times* poll. As in other polls, Wolfe reports, the dividing line is not denominational identity but church attendance. Americans who regularly go to church look at life quite differently from Americans who do not.

"That points to an obvious question: Of the 63 million American Catholics, how many are sufficiently engaged with their Church to satisfy minimum conditions to be a Catholic — or even distinctively religious — presence rather than simply a presence by people who claim a particular denominational identity when talking to a pollster?

"I estimate that somewhere between 10 million and 15 million of the 63 million Catholics actively participate in the Church. Age, health, and other circumstances prevent many from being a public presence in any important sense. Probably somewhere between 5 million and 10 million are able to play this role. That is quite a few people; but it is not the 'presence' that the figure 63 million would suggest."

Hoping to give a somewhat upbeat turn to this rather bleak assessment, I went on to cite two big exceptions to the general rule that "Catholics *qua* Catholic are not an important public presence in America" — the pro-life movement, where Catholics "seem to have shaken off their customary clericalism and entered into coalitions with non-Catholics as a distinctive presence," and inner-city Catholic schools, which, serving as beacons of hope for large numbers of Catholic and non-Catholic children, had supplied "the kind of presence that matters."

Although I did not mention it, neither Catholic involvement in the pro-life movement nor the good work done by

Catholic parochial schools in the inner city is wha
narily be called lay ministry — these are lay apo
although that think-tank session was not the place
of the reason for the general *lack* of Catholic pu
has been the neglect — indeed, virtual abandonment — of organized lay apostolates other than these. In principle, this is not
the fault of the emphasis on lay ministry; but just to the extent
that it supplied a seeming rationale and justification for ignoring apostolate, it contributed to the debacle.

What's in a Name?

Before going further, though, some further explanation will
be in order (without getting bogged down in technicalities, I
hope) concerning the expressions "lay apostolate" and "lay
ministry." Explaining "apostolate" may be especially necessary, since we hear so little about it these days.

The fundamental and hallowed usage of "apostolate" is
stated by theologian William E. May when he writes, "In
essence the term 'apostolate' refers to the mission of the
Church to carry on the redemptive work of Jesus Christ."
Nevertheless, when I use the term "lay apostolate" in this
book, I am referring to something rather more specific: the
efforts of laypeople, whether acting individually on their own
initiative or together with others, to put the truth of the
Gospel into practice in the world through their involvement
in marriage, work, political participation, social relationships,
and all the other legitimate roles and activities of secular life.

Apostolate is not an exercise of political or economic
power, not an attempt to create a theocratic social or political order. It involves no pressure upon or manipulation of
others intended to get them to accept the Gospel or cooperate with Catholic efforts to live out its implications. It is

compatible with, and indeed requires, full respect for the conscientious rights of others in a pluralistic world.

There is an excellent statement of the lay apostolate's grounding in ordinary life near the beginning of the chapter on the laity in Vatican Council II's "Dogmatic Constitution on the Church" (*Lumen Gentium*, 31):

> Their secular character is proper and peculiar to the laity. . . . By reason of their special vocation it belongs to the laity to seek the kingdom of God by engaging in temporal affairs and directing them according to God's will. They live in the world, that is, they are engaged in each and every work and business of the earth and in the ordinary circumstances of social and family life which, as it were, constitute their very existence. There they are called by God that, being led by the spirit to the Gospel, they may contribute to the sanctification of the world, as from within like leaven, by fulfilling their own particular duties.

Plainly, much more could be (and has been) said about lay apostolate than that: about various forms of apostolate, about formation for apostolate, about the apostolate's place in the mission and structure of the Church. We shall go into some of these matters later, with a view to updating earlier statements in light of current realities. But the passage quoted does identify the essential aim of anything properly called lay apostolate: "to seek the kingdom of God by engaging in temporal affairs and directing them according to God's will." That is the essence of lay apostolate as I use the term.

What about lay ministry? As the theologian Father Romanus Cessario, O.P., points out, "ministry" used in the context of referring to the activities of laypeople has an essentially analogical meaning.

That is not to say that what the laity do is inferior, second class, unserious. The word "analogical," as applied to lay ministry, simply means that "ministry" as such is properly the work of bishops, priests, and deacons. This is so even though, as the *Catechism of the Catholic Church* points out (quoting Pope Paul VI's much-praised 1975 apostolic exhortation on evangelization, *Evangelii Nuntiandi*): "The laity can also feel called, or be in fact called, to cooperate with their pastors in the service of the ecclesial community, for the sake of its growth and life. This can be done through the exercise of different kinds of ministries according to the grace and charisms which the Lord has been pleased to bestow on them" (CCC 910).

No one looking at the phenomenon called "lay ministry" as it now exists in the Catholic Church in the United States can help noticing that two very different entities go by this name.

One, as we have seen, is what is called Lay Ecclesial Ministry (LEM) — the work of full- or part-time salaried laypersons in parishes and other ecclesiastical settings who serve as pastoral associates, directors of religious education, liturgical coordinators, social action directors, etc. The other is composed of the activities of a much more numerous body of laymen and laywomen serving on a volunteer basis as eucharistic ministers, cantors, catechists, and in various other roles. The LEMs are Church employees; the volunteer ministers are not. Oddly enough, much that is written and said about lay ministry fails to make this elementary, and extremely important, distinction.

While there are many ways of telling lay apostolate and lay ministry apart, here is a rough-and-ready rule of thumb:

Ministry is something directed to the service of the Church and its members, while apostolate is directed to serving and evangelizing the world. Ministry is "for the sake of [the] growth and life" of the ecclesial community; apostolate is for the enlightenment and well-being of the secular order. Both are needed.

Some discussions of these matters take one word or the other — "apostolate" or "ministry" — as an umbrella term for all forms of participation in the mission of the Church. Today in particular "ministry" often is used that way, while "apostolate" is either not used at all or else is derided as a word from an earlier, now outgrown era in Catholic life.

That is a mistake. It adds to the confusion that comes from indiscriminately calling virtually anything done in an ecclesial setting or for a religious purpose a ministry. "Ministry" is not, and should not become, an all-purpose term of generic approval, a kind of verbal stroking intended to make people feel good about themselves. There are other, better ways of doing that: for instance, giving hard workers public recognition or just saying "thank you" now and then. But the term "ministry" is best reserved for activity that truly is a participation, direct or analogous as the case may be, in the threefold ministry of the clergy: prophet (teacher), priest (sanctifier), king (servant-leader). It takes nothing away from other kinds of generous and useful activity to say that, as good as they are, they aren't ministry.

Another reason for keeping both terms, "apostolate" *and* "ministry," in play and distinct is that this is what the official teaching documents of the Church do. The *Catechism of the Catholic Church*, for example, situates its treatment of apostolate (857-863) before its treatment of ministry (874-878). The *Catechism* makes the point that "the whole Church is apostolic," and quotes from Vatican II's "Decree on the Apostolate of Lay People" (*Apostolicam Actuositatem* is its Latin title): " 'The Christian vocation is, of its nature, a vocation to the apostolate as well.' Indeed, we call an apostolate 'every activity of the Mystical Body' that aims 'to spread the Kingdom of Christ over all the earth' " (863).

For the sake of clear thinking and clear speaking, and perhaps even for the sake of advancing the kingdom of Christ, let us call apostolate *apostolate* and ministry *ministry*, and not mix up the two.

By now, though, someone may be asking: Is all this only an argument about words? Hardly! Some very serious practical matters are at stake here. Just how serious should be clear from the next chapter, which considers the present state of American Catholicism and begins to relate it, as needs to be done, to the story of apostolate and ministry.

TWO

Half Full or Half Empty?

Is the glass half full or half empty? Someone might very well ask that question about Catholicism in the United States. This chapter will try to answer it briefly, and to relate the answer to the central question of this book: ministry or apostolate?

From one point of view, there is a lot to celebrate in American Catholicism.

The Catholic population is very large. For the most part, Catholics are prosperous and successful. Their rate of religious practice is substantially higher than the rate in many similar countries. They give a great deal of money to the Church, and many also give generously of their time and energy. The Church operates an extensive network of schools, hospitals, social service agencies, and other institutions and programs that make a notable contribution to the well-being of countless communities and the nation as a whole. This is a gratifying picture.

Unfortunately, it is not the whole picture. Assessments suggesting otherwise are very wide of the mark. A covering letter accompanying a media kit from the communications department of the Catholic bishops' national conference (prepared and distributed in connection with a "Jubilee Day for Lay Ministers" in November of 2000) offers this example of what I mean: "The Jubilee Day for Lay Ministers comes at a time of incredible growth in the Catholic Church."

With all due respect for the good intentions of whoever wrote that, it just isn't true. In the United States, at least, this is *not* a time of growth, incredible or otherwise, in the Catholic sector. In regard to most matters susceptible of quantitative measurement, the Catholic Church in the United States has been shrinking, not growing, for the last three decades, and it seems to be shrinking now.

During this same period, lay ministry has emerged and flourished, and lay apostolate has declined to the point of all but disappearing. I do *not* mean to assert or suggest a direct cause-and-effect relationship, however. The problems of American Catholicism have *not* been caused by lay ministry nor are they the result — directly, at least — of the decline of apostolate. Yet the contrasting fortunes of apostolate and ministry have been part of the story, ingredients in the mix.

Furthermore, the decline of lay apostolate undoubtedly has played at least a limited role in reducing the Catholic community's capacity to influence American public life and the surrounding culture, besides making it a great deal harder now to change the situation for the better. I'll have more to say about that below.

Before plunging into the bad news, I should underline the fact that I do not subscribe to the gloom-and-doom school of ecclesiastical analysis. As we have seen, there is much to praise in the Church in the United States — much that even now can and should be salvaged. Lay ministry is one of those things. If I did not believe that, I wouldn't be writing this book.

But knee-jerk optimism is no help to facing facts and doing what needs to be done. Since the mid-1960s we have spent too much time hailing the "renewal" of American Catholicism even as significant elements of it were falling down around our ears. Simple, factual honesty about what has happened is a necessary condition for turning things around.

Facing Facts

The notable exception to the general picture of decline in American Catholicism during the last several decades is population. There were 45.6 million Catholics in the United States in 1965 (total U.S population: 190 million); as this is written, in 2001, there officially are a whopping 63 million of us in a total population of some 282 million.

This represents impressive numerical growth, to be sure. But there is much more to be said than that.

One thing that must be said, unfortunately, is that the Catholics of the United States now are served by a notably diminished corps of priests (59,000 in 1965, 46,000 now) and an apparently vanishing corps of religious sisters and brothers (180,000 sisters and 12,000 brothers in 1965 against 81,161 sisters and 5,500 brothers now). Note, though, that there now are also a little under 13,000 permanent deacons in the United States, whereas there were none in 1965.

Between 1965 and 2001, moreover, religious participation by American Catholics as a group declined dramatically. Not surprisingly, the religious knowledge of many is by all accounts sadly deficient ("only a superficial grasp of the essentials of the faith," says Kenneth Woodward, who has written about religion for *Newsweek* since the 1960s). On many issues, the attitudes and behaviors of many of these people are sharply at odds with their own religious tradition.

For example:

- According to Gallup polls, the rate of Sunday Mass attendance by American Catholics reached a high of

74% in 1958, fell to a low of 48% in 1988, and has remained the same since then. Some, however, hold that the Gallup figures are based on a flawed methodology that makes them overly optimistic. According to the Center for Applied Research in the Apostolate, a church-related social science research agency based in Washington, Mass attendance on any given Sunday (or, these days, Sunday plus Saturday evening) now is around 40% of average parish registration — that is to say, about 30% of all the nominal Catholics in the U.S., many of whom are not registered in parishes. CARA puts the actual number at Mass on a typical weekend at 18 million (out of 63 million). "Older Catholics are two to three times as likely as younger Catholics to attend," it says.

- Before Vatican Council II, CARA further reports, about 25% of all sacramental marriages involving Catholics in the U.S. were religiously mixed — Catholics marrying non-Catholics. The number peaked in 1975 at about 37%. Since then, the rate of mixed marriages has dropped — *but so, too, has the rate of sacramental marriage.* In 1970, 20% of all marriages in the U.S. were witnessed by a Catholic priest. In 1980 it was 15% and in 1990, 13%. Also, as is often pointed out, American Catholics now are as likely to get divorces as anybody else.

- The *National Catholic Reporter*, a weekly newspaper of the Catholic left, in October, 1999, published results of public opinion surveys reflecting shifts in the attitudes of American Catholics from 1987 until then. One especially revealing set of questions asked whether it was possible to be a "good Catholic" in various circumstances: without obeying Church teaching on abortion, 39% in 1987, 53% in 1999; and without giving time and money to the poor, 44% and 56%, respectively. Similar majorities said people could be good Catholics without attending Sunday Mass, without giving time and money to their parishes, and while practicing birth control, divorcing and remarrying, and marrying outside the Church. In 1999, in fact, 38% and 23% agreed that it is possible to be a good Catholic without believing, respectively, in Christ's Real Presence in the Eucharist and Christ's physical resurrection from the dead. "As we scan from the pre-Vatican II to the post-Vatican II generation," sociologist James D. Davidson remarked, "we find less and less attachment to the church."

And, all that aside, there is the disquieting fact noted by *Newsweek*'s Woodward:

If we are to talk about overlooked stories, my chief candidate is how the Catholic Church has become the farm system for other Christian denominations. If it weren't for disaffected Catholics, there would be half the number of Episcopalians [about 2.3 million at last count]. Without former Catholics, a lot of local, non-denominational "community" churches would have to disband, or might not even exist. Who stays, who leaves and why — these questions have not been thoroughly studied.

Opinions differ on the answers to those questions, but the fact is beyond dispute: The old joke that Catholics are the largest religious body in the United States and ex-Catholics the second largest appears to be unpleasantly close to the truth. Whatever else it may be, for American Catholicism this is not "a time of incredible growth."

Nor, unfortunately, is there much reason for optimism about Catholic conflicts and divisions, such as that expressed in a booklet published by the Common Ground Initiative. Common Ground is a project launched by the late Cardinal Joseph Bernardin of Chicago shortly before his death in 1996 with the praiseworthy aim of bringing Catholic conservatives and liberals together in dialogue. But useful dialogue has to start from sounder grounds than the assertion, in this 1999 publication, that "so-called liberals, conservatives, progressives, and neo-conservatives share with the people in the pews 99.9 percent of a distinctive world view."

Leave aside the fact that the writer speaks of consensus on a "world view" rather than a body of religious truth: Even on its own terms, the assertion is very dubious. The elements of this world view supposedly shared by Catholics spanning the ideological spectrum from left to right are said to include such things as "conviction of the inherent nature of human dignity and the sanctity of life," belief in "the priority of the transcendent . . . in human affairs," and "an attitude of obedience and even awe toward the church."

Once again, the facts are very different from what is being claimed. The National Opinion Research Center reported in early 1999 that the number of Catholics who called their attachment to the Church "strong" had fallen from 46% in the 1970s to 37% by that time, while the number claiming to attend Mass weekly dropped from 48% to 29%. Also, according to NORC, 51% of Catholics approved of abortion in some circumstances and 31% for any reason at all; 67% supported capital punishment; 48% said premarital sex is "not wrong at all" compared with only 21% who called it always wrong; and 57% held that birth control should be available to teenagers even if their parents disapprove.

Bear in mind that many of the issues implicated in findings like these are not questions of personal belief and private morality; attitudes on civic morality and public policy are involved in many instances. This points strongly to the conclusion that American Catholics as a group are ill-equipped to play a positive role *precisely as Catholics* in the shaping of culture.

Stephen J. Pope, a Boston College theologian, says the "vast majority" of Catholics, including graduates of Catholic colleges and universities, are only "vaguely aware" of natural law and have probably never read a papal social encyclical. Most, too, he says, have probably never heard of such figures as Monsignor John Ryan, the educator and activist who did so much to shape the Church's social doctrine and social policy in America in the early decades of the twentieth century; Father John Courtney Murray, S.J., the theologian who helped usher in a new era in Catholic thinking about church and state and religious liberty in the 1950s and 1960s; and Jacques Maritain, the French Catholic philosopher (he taught for many years in the United States) whose writings on Christian humanism and the Christian's role in the secular order had a powerful influence on the Second Vatican Council.

Dr. Pope underlines the fact, especially important in the present context, that the falling-off in Mass attendance by Catholics is a matter of concern not just because of its implications for their personal spirituality but because of what it implies for their public role. He points out:

> Just as we might worry about people "bowling alone,"
> we ought also to be concerned about Catholics engaged
> in "praying alone" as a New Age substitute for church

membership. The decline in churchgoing among Catholics is a serious issue. One of its consequences will be the diminished impact of Catholicism on our civic life. English sociologist Robin Gill has shown convincingly that lower church attendance correlates significantly with lower adherence to Christian beliefs and lower levels of identification with Christian morality. If the same trend obtains in the United States, one can expect a decline of Catholic identification with the Church's moral teachings, including those pertaining to social morality.

These painful facts and disconcerting trends are part of the real-life background for the decline of lay apostolate and the rise of lay ministry during the last several decades.

Apostolate's Fall, Ministry's Rise

In speaking about the laity, Vatican Council II spoke mostly about apostolate. It defined the special role of laypeople in the Church's mission in relation to their involvement in the affairs of the secular world. Declaring "the apostolate of the laity" to be "a sharing in the salvific mission of the Church," the Council's "Dogmatic Constitution on the Church" (*Lumen Gentium*, 33), said:

> Through Baptism and Confirmation all are appointed to this apostolate by the Lord himself. Moreover, by the sacraments, and especially by the Eucharist, that love of God and man which is the soul of the apostolate is communicated and nourished. The laity, however, are given this special vocation: to make the Church present and fruitful in those places and circumstances where it is only through them that she can become the salt of the earth.

The Council also opened the door to lay ministry, saying in the very next paragraph that laypeople have "the capacity of being appointed by the hierarchy to some ecclesiastical offices with a view to a spiritual end" (*Lumen Gentium*, 33). But in the eyes of Vatican II, the distinctive feature of the laity is their sharing in the Church's mission through their participation in secular life; this sharing is lay apostolate. Lay ministry occupies a somewhat subordinate place. The "Decree on the Apostolate of Lay People" points out that "the characteristic of the lay state" is "a life led in the midst of the world and of secular affairs"; that, it says, is where laypeople are called to the apostolate (*Apostolicam Actuositatem*, 2).

An important development in the emergence of lay ministry occurred in 1972, when Pope Paul VI did away with the so-called "minor orders" and the subdiaconate, which had been stages on the way to ordination, first as a deacon and then as a priest, and assigned the liturgical functions of subdeacons to the lay ministries of lector and acolyte. In doing so, Pope Paul also invited other lay ministries. "Ministries may be committed to lay Christians," he said. "They are no longer to be regarded as reserved to candidates for the sacrament of Orders."

Paul VI's action undoubtedly gave important impetus to the growth of lay ministry. At the same time, there is no reason to believe it was meant to cancel or weaken what Vatican Council II had said just a short time before about lay apostolate — that it is the proper and distinctive way in which Catholic laypeople participate in the Church's mission.

The Magisterium of the Church has repeated this message many times over the years. Pope John Paul II returns to it in his broad-ranging document "The Lay Members of Christ's Faithful People" (*Christifideles Laici*, 2), which sums up the 1987 world Synod of Bishops on the laity. But there he also speaks of something else — the "difficulties and dangers" attending the path of the laity in the postconciliar years.

> In particular, two temptations can be cited which they [the laity] have not always known how to avoid: the temptation of being so strongly interested in Church services and tasks that some fail to become actively engaged in their responsibilities in the professional, social, cultural and political world; and the temptation of legitimizing the unwarranted separation of faith from life, that is, a separation of the Gospel's acceptance from the actual living of the Gospel in various situations in the world.

Clearly he judges both to be temptations to betray the "prophetic significance" of Vatican II's teaching. The first temptation is for laypeople to get bogged down in ministries and neglect apostolate; the second is for them to separate faith (with ministries) from life (without apostolate).

Very soon after the Council, however, an upsurge of interest began in the subject of "ministry" in general and lay ministry in particular. Some of it can be traced to the work of the Belgian theologian Edward Schillebeeckx, O.P. The American theologian Romanus Cessario, O.P., points out that the Congregation for the Doctrine of the Faith took "strong exception" to some of Father Schillebeeckx's writing for not acknowledging the doctrinal principle that all authentic ministry derives from the bishop, especially the Bishop of Rome.

"The large numbers of lay pastoral workers or associates who have begun to assist in areas of Europe where there is a shortage of ordained priests has given a certain impetus to this theological reflection," Father Cessario remarks dryly.

Something similar has happened in the United States during these years, though up to now probably not as widely or with the same intensity of problematical theological reflection as in Europe.

Over time, the apostolate of the laity was more and more neglected, both in theory and in practice. The organizational and institutional infrastructure of lay apostolate in American Catholicism was largely dismantled as part of the dismantling of the Catholic subculture begun in the late 1950s and continued at an accelerated pace in the 1960s and on into the 1970s. (We shall examine these matters more closely in the next chapter.) By the time it was over, "lay apostolate" was more nearly a historical term than the name of a living reality in the Church in the U.S.

As lay apostolate waned, lay ministry waxed. There were landmarks along the way.

One was the publication in 1980 by the National Conference of Catholic Bishops of a statement entitled "Called and Gifted." Reflecting the interests of the NCCB committee on the laity and the corresponding lay staff of the bishops' conference, it placed an episcopal stamp of approval upon the idea of lay ministry.

Curiously enough, while de facto giving a major boost to lay ministry *in the Church*, "Called and Gifted" was supposedly issued to mark the fifteenth anniversary of Vatican Council II's "Decree on the Apostolate of Lay People," which emphasized apostolate *in the world* as the laity's special work. The American document focused on four "calls" that it said laypeople should respond to: the call to adulthood, the call to holiness, the call to community, and the call to ministry. This latter call was said to come from the sacraments of baptism and confirmation, which "empower all believers to share in some form of ministry," with the particular form for each determined by his or her individual gifts.

The document also took specific note of a new development: the emergence of lay ecclesial ministers. Although volunteer part-time ministers were said also to be involved in ecclesial ministry along with the lay ecclesial ministers, it was pointed out that the latter were engaged in *professional* ministry. This makes it hard to tell whether "Called and Gifted" was talking about two different things or one single thing with two distinct subdivisions. But the overall message was clear: Ministry was in, apostolate was out.

Another important publication, three years later, was a book called *Theology of Ministry*, by Father Thomas Franklin O'Meara, O.P. Arguing that it had become "*de rigueur* for everyone to be in ministry," this University of Notre Dame theologian conceded that the rise of ministry was "not dictated by the Council" nor the result of a conscious policy choice by the Church; instead, he announced, it was "part of a cultural upheaval whose roots lie in a search for freedom, ministerial efficacy, maturity and social equality within the Church."

Theology of Ministry has been influential in elite circles eager to push ministry. A *National Catholic Reporter* review of a revised edition, published in 2000, says the book "became a standard text in many seminaries and new lay ministry programs at a time when ministry in the church was evolving and expanding so rapidly that even official church policy adopted a wait-and-see stance."

In 1995 the U.S. bishops returned to the subject of lay ministry in yet another statement, "Called and Gifted for the Third Millennium." One concrete result of this document was the establishment by the NCCB Committee on the Laity of a special subcommittee on lay ministry whose purpose was, as it explained later, "to come to a better understanding of the range of issues concerning lay ministry in the church in the United States; given a deepened understanding of them, to bring certain issues to the attention of the episcopal conference; and to offer options for addressing them."

A Report and a Declaration

Chaired by Bishop Phillip F. Straling of Reno, Nevada, the subcommittee reported back to the U.S. bishops at their general meeting in Washington, D.C., in November, 1999. The printed report, a document entitled "Lay Ecclesial Ministry: State of the Questions," gave the following helpful overview of developments in the previous twenty years.

During this time, the American bishops collectively had "focused on laypersons serving in Church ministries." This focusing included the two pastoral statements mentioned above — "Called and Gifted" and "Called and Gifted for the Third Millennium" — and two research studies on people engaged in parish pastoral ministry, as well the activities of the subcommittee itself.

The subcommittee saluted "Called and Gifted" for having recognized relatively early in the game (1980) "a new development since the Second Vatican Council" — namely, that laypeople had started serving as part-time workers and volunteers on pastoral councils and other advisory boards and as eucharistic ministers, lectors, catechists, pastoral assistants, and missionaries. Moreover, laypeople preparing for professional work in the Church received "special mention" as ecclesial ministers. Adding that many of these ecclesial ministers were hired by parishes, diocesan offices, and Church agencies to fill staff positions and were given significant leadership responsibilities, the subcommittee on lay ministry said that it meant "to focus specifically on this group."

The subcommittee recalled that the first national research study of lay ecclesial ministers commissioned by the bishops appeared in 1992 with the title *New Parish Ministers: Laity and Religious on Parish Staffs*. The author, Monsignor Philip J. Murnion of the National Pastoral Life Center in New York, estimated that 21,500 laypeople were working full- or part-time in "formal pastoral roles." The figure did not include support and maintenance staff and parochial schoolteachers. But, strange to say, the figure of 21,500 *lay*persons did include "vowed religious" — mostly, religious sisters. (The bishops' conference insists on counting sisters working on parish staffs among the *lay* ecclesial ministers. This is canonically correct — religious are not clerics, so by process of elimination they must be laity. But hardly anybody thinks of them that way, including the religious themselves. The number of religious who are "lay" ministers is dropping in any case, as — unfortunately — their numbers overall decline.)

A follow-up study, *Parishes and Parish Ministers*, by Monsignor Murnion and David DeLambo, was published in 1999. By then, the number of lay ecclesial ministers had risen to 29,145, an increase of 35%. About 60% of U.S. parishes employed lay ministers at that time. Such personnel also could be found in hospitals and other health-care institutions, educational institutions, prisons, and seaport and airport ministries; the number in settings like these was at least thirty-five hundred as of 1996.

The subcommittee said that in the 1995 NCCB statement on the laity, "Called and Gifted for the Third Millennium," the bishops had provided "a more complete description of lay ministries" and had pledged to expand their study and dialogue concerning lay ministry. The creation of the lay ministry subcommittee was one immediate practical result.

The report gave this account of the subcommittee's work: "Our project set out to focus specifically on this group of lay ministers [that is, the salaried lay ecclesial ministers working in parishes and some other institutional settings]. However, we have struggled with the knowledge that the boundaries that distinguish ecclesial ministers from other lay ministers and from all the laity are flexible and permeable; there is no universally accepted delineation." The rest of the report describes this struggling and the questions to which it gave rise in the subcommittee's mind — for the most part, questions of definition and job description.

While "Lay Ecclesial Ministry: State of the Questions," taken as a whole, is a less than memorable literary work, it does contain important information — and also this important, and in some ways troubling, remark:

> One element of the unique character of the laity, within
> the one mission of the Church, is its secular character.
> Because of this secular character, the laity are the Church
> in the heart of the world and bring the world into the
> heart of the Church. The laity's missionary activity in
> the world is sometimes referred to as an apostolate.

In fact, for many years the laity's "missionary activity in the world" was universally called apostolate. As we have seen, this was the word used for it by the Second Vatican Council, which made a clear distinction between lay apostolate and the ministerial roles of some laypeople. The diffident language of the bishops' subcommittee perhaps suggests a certain embarrassment in the face of these matters of fact, which unavoidably stand in stark contrast with its own emphasis on the "lay ecclesial ministry" of a very few.

The report continued:

> All of the laity are called to work toward the transformation of the secular world. Some do this by working in the secular realm; others do this by working in the Church and focusing on the building of ecclesial communion, which has as its ultimate purpose the transformation of the world. Lay ecclesial ministry should not be seen as a retreat by the laity from their role in the secular realm. Rather, lay ecclesial ministry is an affirmation that the Spirit can call the lay faithful to participation in the building of the Church in various ways.

Not only is this confused, but it is confused in ways that can only be disturbing to someone who wants to take bishops' documents seriously.

For one thing, is the purpose of lay ministry "the building of the Church" (that seems about right) or "the transformation of the world" (the sphere of lay apostolate, not of lay ministry)? On a deeper level, one might note that the "ultimate purpose" of ecclesial communion is *not* the transformation of the world. Ecclesial communion is divine-human communion, the incipient kingdom of God; so the ultimate end of ecclesial communion is no less than the fullness of the kingdom itself. Even the visible aspect of ecclesial communion is the salvation of humankind, not just the transformation of the world (although humankind's complete salvation does indeed include the world's transformation).

Leaving these matters aside, nevertheless, the passage is attempting to make a helpful point, which would be even more helpful if it were stated clearly: Somehow or other, the work of the laity participating in the mission of the Church out in the secular world (apostolate) comes before the work that some do in church settings (ministry), in the sense that it is what is proper to and distinctive about laypeople in relation to the Church's mission.

Considering things in this light, it is remarkable that, for two decades during which the bishops' conference of the United States devoted substantial time and resources to lay ministry (and in particular to a very small group of lay ecclesial ministers who include religious sisters), it said and did virtually nothing to encourage and promote lay apostolate. The Catholic laity's participation in the mission of the Church in and to the secular world largely disappeared from the agenda of the bishops' national organization, as it did from the agendas of many dioceses, parishes, and Church institutions and groups. This was strange, to say the least.

And now? As an illustration of the way the idea of ministry currently dominates people's thinking about what committed laity should be doing, a lay friend of mine notes the proliferation of parish "ministry fairs" designed to introduce parishioners to the various service activities open to them and encourage them to sign up. There is nothing wrong with this of course — except for the reinforcement it gives to the notion that "ministry" within the parish setting is what really *good* Catholics do. "The only negative homily you are likely to hear all year is the one blaming people who are not involved in some ministry," this person remarks.

A Declaration of Concern

Well over twenty years ago, it already had become apparent — at least to some — that a wrong turn had been taken. In December, 1977, forty-seven prominent Catholics issued a statement called "A Chicago Declaration of Christian Concern." The link to Chicago was significant, not just because the signers hailed from there but because, in the years before Vatican II, the Archdiocese of Chicago had enjoyed a national reputation as the birthplace and home to numerous lay apostolic organizations and movements widely recognized as a source of important dynamism in American Catholicism.

The Chicago Declaration "hit a nerve," according to one commentary. Conferences, radio programs, and scores of articles discussed the points it raised; nearly two million copies eventually were distributed, and a secretariat called the National Center for the Laity (still in existence) was established to carry on its work. Much that the Declaration said remains relevant and important today.

Noting that there had been a concentration on "internal issues" in the Church since Vatican II, the document complained that "the laity who spend most of their time and energy in the professional and occupational world appear to have been deserted." It then asked: "Who now sustains lay persons as they meet the daily challenges of their job and profession — the arena in which questions of justice and peace are really located? Where are the movements and organizations supporting the young toward a Christian maturity?"

As the Chicago Declaration saw it, such movements and organizations had disappeared. What had taken their place — to the extent anything had — was lay ministry. And although the involvement of laypeople in Church ministries was a good thing in principle, it also seemed in danger of going off the track.

The tendency has been to see lay ministry as involvement in some Church related activity, e.g., religious education, pastoral care for the sick or elderly, or readers in church on Sunday. Thus lay ministry is seen as participation in work traditionally assigned to priests or religious. . . . Such ideas clearly depart from the mainstream of Catholic social thought which regards the advance of social justice as essentially the service performed within one's professional and occupational milieu.

Without holding up the lay apostolic movements of earlier days as models fully adequate to the needs of Church and society in the postconciliar years, the Declaration nevertheless expressed regret over the decline and disappearance of these groups that had formerly done good and important work. Nothing better had come along to take their place, it said, and the result appeared to be "the loss of a generation of Catholic leadership." Recall that this was 1977. A quartercentury later, we can speak of the loss of two generations — and working on a third.

The Chicago Declaration of Christian Concern concluded:

> In the last analysis, the Church speaks to and acts upon the world through her laity. . . . No amount of social action by priests and religious can ever be an adequate substitute for enhancing lay responsibility. The absence of lay initiative can only take us down the road to clericalism. We are deeply concerned that so little energy is devoted to encouraging and arousing lay responsibility for the world. The Church must constantly be reformed, but we fear that the almost obsessive preoccupation with the Church's structures and processes has diverted attention from the essential question: reform for what purpose? It would be one of the great ironies of history

if the era of Vatican II which opened the windows of the Church were to close with a Church turned in upon itself.

This warning remains true today.

But even though it does, as I reread these words of a group of concerned Catholics a quarter-century ago, I cannot help wondering whether people who are younger than I am or have shorter memories will see their point. "The Church is as it is," someone might say, "and it has always been like this, has it not? 'Ministry' is the name of the game for lay people who want to be involved. 'Apostolate' — what's that?"

If I am right and that is *really* how some readers of this book are likely to react to what has been said so far, then to understand how the Church in the United States got into its present bind, as well as how it might get out, we shall need to spend some time looking at history. The chapter that follows tells the story of the lay apostolate.

THREE

'With Pennons Flying'

Confession is good for the soul. Here is mine.

In 1951 I spent the better part of a week in New York attending a Summer School of Catholic Action ("SSCA" for short). The confession is this: I was there for New York, not Catholic Action.

Despite having attained the sophisticated age of sixteen, I had never visited New York. Obviously I was not meant to suffer such deprivation. So, when my Jesuit high school in Washington had begun talking up the summer school a few months earlier, it struck me as a good way of filling this particular gap — especially since the reassurance that I would be immersed in Catholic Action made it easy for me to sell the idea of a trip to New York to my devout, economy-minded mother.

And there I was, passing a week on the campus of Fordham University up in the Bronx with several hundred other adolescents of both sexes from Catholic high schools up and down the East Coast. In those years, similar sessions were held over the summer at other Jesuit campuses around the country. The participants were assumed to be the young Catholic leaders of the future, hungry for indoctrination in the lay apostolate.

No doubt that is what most of them were. As for me, I was hungry to see New York.

Slipping off the Fordham campus just about every evening and riding the Third Avenue elevated train into the heart of Manhattan, I took in the sights — Empire State Building, Rockefeller Center, Times Square, everything else I could. I ate in an Automat. I went to the movies. I attended a Broadway show — a musical version of Booth Tarkington's "Seventeen" that dazzled me. Unbeknownst to me, *The Catcher in the Rye* had been published just a short time before; but my New York bore little resemblance to troubled Holden Caulfield's. I had a grand and glorious week.

Even so, wanting to play fair (with my parents who had paid for the trip, and the Jesuits who had encouraged me to take it), I put in my days out there in the Bronx at the summer school. What did I learn? After many years, only general impressions remain, and they are decidedly mixed.

By today's standards the message of the SSCA would seem hopelessly narrow and naïve. Here was a version of Catholicism at once triumphalistic and defensive, to the point of paranoia. I recall a class on the apostolate of the written word (I fancied myself a budding writer) where the examples commended to us as literary titans were Catholic authors of decidedly minor stature. As I recollect it, the indispensable criterion of titanship in this small world was unquestioning loyalty to the Catholic Church.

But I also encountered something else at the SSCA — something sound and admirable. Whether it was put into words or not I don't recall, but that part of the message quite plainly went like this: "You young people have the good fortune to be Catholics who are free to study and practice your faith. You have received a great gift. You owe a lot in return.

The world desperately needs what you have been given — the truth and life of Jesus Christ. Your parents, your teachers, and your Church expect great things of you. Go out and win the world for Christ!"

One of the features of the SSCA, much ballyhooed to us kids before the event, was the presence of Father Daniel A. Lord, S.J. An activist Jesuit who as director of the Sodality of the Blessed Virgin had made it the largest Catholic youth organization in the United States, Father Lord was the founder of the summer schools. In 1951 he was an elderly man and quite possibly in poor health (he was to die four years later). He was said to have a knack for talking to young people. But even though I was prepared to fall under his spell, I went away from the few crowded sessions at which he talked to us and played the piano — a small figure in black on a stage at a great distance — wondering what all the fuss was about. Another confession, I suppose.

I had no idea then, of course, but two decades earlier, a year after the launching of the SSCA, Father Lord had published an article in *America* magazine providing a cogent account of the thinking behind the new project. The members of the Catholic hierarchy, he wrote, were "trained through long years for the apostolic mission," and laypeople could hardly hope to collaborate effectively with them — as Catholic Action wanted them to do — without "a somewhat proportionate training."

> Catholicism cannot be applied to the whole of life without considerable thought and practical experience. The Encyclicals dealing with Catholic Action are sufficiently packed with thought and suggested work to demand thoughtful study. And if leaders for Catholic Action were

to be developed . . . they needed a training that made clear what Catholic Action meant, what were the actual apostolic possibilities of lay men and women, [and] how existing organizations could be adjusted to cooperate in the high purposes of the Holy Father or the frequently expressed wishes of the ecclesiastical leaders of America.

Little though I suspected it, this vision, shared by Daniel Lord and many other Catholics of those days, was responsible for bringing me to the Fordham campus in the summer of 1951.

In some ways, of course, it was a very old idea.

From Diognetus to Modern Times

Just how old becomes clear when we go back beyond the 1950s and even the 1930s — all the way back to the year 200, when an anonymous Christian writer addressed a letter to a high-ranking pagan who had asked for an account of the new religion, Christianity, which was then the subject of conflicting reports, many of them suspicious and hostile. This document has come down to us as the Epistle to Diognetus. In some respects it has never been bettered as an exposition of the role of Christians in the world.

Christians are not distinguished from the rest of mankind by either country, speech, or customs; the fact is, they nowhere settle in cities of their own; they use no peculiar language; they cultivate no eccentric mode of life. . . . Yet while they dwell in both Greek and non-Greek cities, as each one's lot was cast, and conform to the customs of the country in dress, food, and mode of life in general, the whole tenor of their way of living stamps it as worthy of admiration and admittedly extraordinary. They reside in their respective countries, but only as aliens. They take part in everything as citizens and put up with everything as foreigners. Every foreign land is their home, and every home a foreign land. They marry like all others and beget children; but they do not expose their offspring. Their board they spread for all, but not their bed. They find themselves in the flesh, but do not live according to the flesh. They spend their days on earth, but hold citizenship in heaven. They obey the established laws, but in their private lives they rise above the laws. They love all men, but are persecuted by all. They are unknown, yet are condemned; they are put to death, but it is life they receive. They are poor, and enrich many. . . . In a word: what the soul is in the body, that the Christians are in the world.

Idealized though this may have been, it did correspond to a reality. In that time and place, the Roman Empire of the early third century, the marginalization and occasional persecution to which Christians were exposed made being a Christian no easy thing. Those who persevered gave testimony simply by persevering.

Inevitably this changed as Christianity came to be, first, tolerated and then established in the centuries that followed. Drastic alterations in society accompanied the dissolution of the Empire in the West. And a long eclipse set in for the laity.

During the Middle Ages, the comparatively small number of powerful lay lords did try to take over the Church by controlling the selection of bishops and other Church officials. But apart from this practice of "lay investiture" (as it was called), the general drift of the whole period was to exclude laypeople from the affairs of the Church and create a diminished sense of lay participation in the Church's mission.

The late Bishop Alvaro del Portillo, formerly prelate of the Opus Dei prelature, summed it up like this: "The layman found his field of action reduced to worldly affairs, with the disappearance of the sense of the laity's participation in the field proper to the Church, which had been so lively in the early centuries; the Church's mission came to be identified almost exclusively with the ministry of clerics." Developments during the era of the Reformation and Counter-Reformation in the sixteenth century tended to reinforce this state of affairs.

There were some hints of change in the nineteenth century. But the really dramatic changes came in the century that followed. Far and away the most dramatic, in the early years of the twentieth century, was Catholic Action.

The High Noon of Catholic Action

In the United States, Catholic Action is only a name in the history books today. But here as elsewhere, it was once very important indeed: a cutting-edge movement that sought, for the first time in a millennium and a half, to motivate and form Catholic laypeople to play an active role in the mission of the Church. It was identified especially with Pope Pius IX (pope from 1922 to 1939), but was enthusiastically promoted by popes before and after him, too.

Church leaders saw Catholic Action as a way of inserting the message of the Gospel into the structures of an increasingly dechristianized secular world through the agency of the laity acting at the bishops' behest. And, as hindsight now makes clear, there was its great weakness — the inhibiting factor that was built into the very understanding of "Catholic Action." Time and again its most ardent proponents, from the pope on down, unblushingly explained that Catholic Action meant participation by the laity *in the apostolate of the hierarchy*. That laypeople had their own proper role to play in the Church's mission — a role that was not a form of participation in anyone else's apostolate — occurred to hardly anybody.

I once encountered a man who had been a leader in Catholic Action in Canada years before and who maintained that, in his experience, laypeople involved in Catholic Action had acted independently and not (as was sometimes said) as the "long arm" of the hierarchy. I was glad to hear it. But all the same the official literature regularly took a very different view: Catholic Action *was* the laity's sharing in something proper to bishops and priests. Partly, at least, that was the source of its eventual undoing.

In its day, nevertheless, Catholic Action was a great thing, marking significant progress in thinking about laypeople. "Catholic Action is life and living inspired and filled by the teaching and the power of Christ," wrote Father John J. Burke, C.S.P., general secretary of the National Catholic Welfare Conference (predecessor of today's United States Conference of Catholic Bishops). In a 1931 article he explained:

> Catholic action means the living, the showing, the carrying forward of Christ in our living hearts and our living bodies — into the kingdom of Christ. The field of that kingdom is anything and everything human. . . . Catholic action is, therefore, a knowledge, an ever-increasing knowledge of the faith that is in us, of its consequences, its social relations and obligations.

Two years later Father John LaFarge, S.J., a pioneer in the Catholic interracial movement and other social action movements in the Church in the United States, reported in a periodical called *Social Justice Bulletin* on the New York convention of the National Catholic Alumni Federation and speculated on how, in the spirit of Catholic Action, graduates of Catholic colleges and universities could play an important role in the Depression-era reshaping of American society. Quoting an official of the federal National Recovery Administration, he wrote:

> The task now facing our graduates . . . is "to find a democratic and a truly American solution of the problem that has produced dictatorships in at least three great nations since the World War.". . . Our bulwark against dictatorships is the ethical heritage that we enjoy as Catholics through our Church and as Americans through our Constitution. We look to the Catholic graduate to apply this heritage to the opportunity now at hand.

This must have been heady stuff for a Catholic graduate who was the child or grandchild of immigrants from Ireland or Bavaria, Poland, Italy, or Slovakia, or someplace else where his forebears for many generations had been peasants or laborers.

Even now, there is much to admire in the best thinking about Catholic Action: the persistent linking of liturgy and life in the world, including action for justice, the idea of the Church as Mystical Body of Christ, the understanding of the lay vocation as rooted in the baptismal priesthood. Such themes often appeared in the pages of *Orate Fratres*, a leading publication of the liturgical movement. As in this 1931 editorial:

Catholic Action or Lay Apostolate is the great need of the age. It embodies the hopes of the Vicar of Christ for a spiritual regeneration of the world. Its inspiration and strength lie in the royal priesthood of the laity. . . . Every Catholic should be an apostle, a missionary of Christ. . . . As branches of Christ, as members of His Church and children of God we are bound to love God above all and our neighbor as ourselves. . . . As we are all one with and in Christ, Christ will reward all the good that we do to our neighbor, as if we had done it to Himself.

Twenty years later, I heard the same message at the Summer School of Catholic Action.

Hardly Perfect, Not So Bad

It would be wrong to romanticize the Catholic Action of those days or make it out to have been better than it was. For one thing, it was far from being universally understood and embraced. Writing in the late 1930s, Graham Greene remarked of Catholic Action that "the Vatican has been many years ahead of the bishops and the laity — for years the Pope [Pius XI] has had to meet a kind of passive resistance from the Church." It also could be shrill and defensive, obsessed with battling the Church's enemies, usually identified as secularists, atheists, and/or communists. Military images were common, as in a 1931 editorial in *Catholic Apostolate*:

The second phase of Catholic Action is demonstrative and aggressive. Its scope is not only to repel the enemy but to sally forth with pennons flying to make new conquests for Christ. . . . They, the pagans, set all manner of organizations afoot to attract the young and imbue

49

them with their fads that lack enduring value — aye, which very often are shamelessly indecent or downright hostile to religion. Obviously it ill becomes us to stand by inarticulate with folded arms. We too must be up and doing.

And so on. Like the little girl in the rhyme, when Catholic Action was good, it was very, very good, but when it was bad, it was horrid.

But whether it was horrid or good, at least it was more than homilies and editorials, more than words. In the years before Vatican Council II, the lay apostolate in the United States — not only Catholic Action but all the rest of it — was organized around a remarkable infrastructure of Church-sponsored institutions and organizations.

As with the rest of this story, it is important not to succumb to nostalgia and exaggerate the merits of all this. An editorial in the lay-edited magazine *Commonweal*, appearing in 1964 at the tail end of the period in question, noted that the more than three hundred Catholic groups it then could find in existence included such as the Catholic Accountants Guild, the Catholic Aviation League of Our Lady of Loreto, and the International Federation of Middle Class Catholics.

Complaining of the "defensiveness" of Catholic groups, the magazine accused them of "clannishness designed to prevent attrition from the Church" and of perpetuating lay dependence on the clergy and immaturity of faith. The need now, as the Church prepared to move into the era after Vatican II, was "fully aware Christians who will . . . work on their own to create a more Christian environment."

As a critique of many Catholic lay groups before the Council, this contains a measure of truth along with a substantial measure of exaggeration and caricature. In view of what soon was to happen — indeed, even then *was* happening — it can be seen now as overkill.

Furthermore, organizations with a clannish mindset were hardly the only ones on the Catholic scene. For instance, there also was the "small but vigorous network of Catholic Action groups centered in the Midwest" of which historian David O'Brien writes, with their emphasis on "the social-action orientation and formation of laypersons for work in the secular world." It is these that the 1977 Chicago Declaration of Christian Concern spoke of in referring regretfully to "the decline and, too often, the demise of those organizations and networks of the recent past whose task it was to inspire and support Christians in their vocation to the world through their professional and occupational lives."

The Declaration explained that it meant groups like the National Catholic Social Action Conference, the National Conference of Christian Employers and Managers, the Association of Catholic Trade Unionists, the National Council of Catholic Nurses, Young Christian Students, Young Christian Workers, and the Catholic Council on Working Life. Further to the left, the Chicago document might have added, was the New York-based Catholic Worker Movement, founded by Dorothy Day and Peter Maurin; although never numerically large, it provided a spiritual stimulus to a number of Catholic activists and intellectuals of the day.

Since Vatican II, the Chicago Declaration acknowledged, concern for justice and peace had become more prominent on the agenda of the ecclesiastical bureaucracy than it had been in the years when organizations like these flourished. Nevertheless, it saw "no evidence that such bureaucratization has led to further involvement of lay Christians."

In sum, during their heyday — roughly the three decades leading up to the Second Vatican Council — lay groups and movements of all sorts were a prominent part of American Catholicism. It hardly needs saying that not all of them were dynamic embodiments of the best in the Catholic tradition. Some no doubt deserved the sneers aimed at them by the intellectuals at *Commonweal* and other strongholds of the Catholic left. But, on the whole, they were a notable achievement just the same. By the middle years of the twentieth century they had helped to make Catholicism, in Charles Morris's words, "a dominant, possibly the dominant, religious and cultural influence in the country."

It would have made good sense to reform and renew many of these lay groups and movements in light of Vatican II's new insights about the laity and their place in the Church's mission. Instead, they were pretty much abandoned. From the late 1950s through the mid-1970s, this remarkable organizational infrastructure shrank to a shadow of what it had been. It is crucial to understand what happened and why.

Collapsing the Subculture

It began before Vatican II, and, to a surprising extent, it was the result of a deliberate choice: a choice spearheaded by Catholics themselves. An important turning point was the publication in 1955 (in a now-defunct Fordham journal called *Thought*) of an article entitled "American Catholics and the Intellectual Life." Written by Monsignor John Tracy Ellis, a respected Church historian at the Catholic University of America, it had the effect in certain circles, Morris records, of "a match in an oxygen tent."

The article's theme was the intellectual mediocrity of American Catholics and their institutions, including Catholic colleges and universities. The indictment was backed up with what Morris calls "a thudding litany of Catholic failure."

The Catholic intellectual elite rushed to clamber on board this new bandwagon. I remember an excited lay professor at my Jesuit university, Georgetown, proselytizing a classroom full of uncomprehending undergraduates with the good news of this revelation; he and others like him on Catholic campuses across the nation were engaged in launching what was to become a prolonged exercise in public self-flagellation by educated Catholics for the supposed intellectual sins of their Church.

Strange to say, much of this self-criticism was out of date by the time it became popular to indulge in it. The notion of Catholic intellectual backwardness, however accurate it might have been twenty or thirty years earlier, no longer corresponded to the facts; as Charles Morris points out, measured by almost all standard socioeconomic indices Catholics were "almost precisely at the national white median score by the 1960s, and substantially above average by the 1970s." By then, too, Catholics outperformed Protestants and were approaching the performance of Jews in higher education. But the Tracy Ellis thesis was widely accepted as Gospel truth.

And it was acted upon. Part of that involved the dismantling of the American Catholic subculture. This remarkable infrastructure — parishes, hospitals, schools, colleges, and universities, along with a vast array of organizations and movements — had been built up painstakingly by American Catholics at enormous cost and with commendable devotion over the previous century. Despite its limitations, it was a source of great strength. In a few years, it was largely gone.

Partly this happened through the efforts of Catholic intellectuals suffering from feelings of inferiority and eager to acquire the respect of nonbelieving peers. But only partly. It was also a result of demographic and cultural factors that the intellectuals had done nothing to create, notably including the breakdown of tightly knit ethnic neighborhoods, often organized around parish churches, as a result of the large-scale movement of Catholics and others to the new post-World War II suburbs. Needless to say, the results of this shift were both unanticipated and overwhelming for the Church.

Here, then, was the "fearsome exercise" of which Morris speaks: "the dangerous and potentially catastrophic project of severing the connection between the Catholic religion and the separatist American Catholic culture that had always been the source of its dynamism, its appeal, and its power."

The result, says social scientist Joseph A. Varacalli (in an angry book called *Bright Promise, Failed Community*), has been a "debacle." Along with the rest of the infrastructure of American Catholicism, Catholic lay organizations naturally fell victim to this self-inflicted Catholic *Kulturkampf*, often ironically carried out after Vatican II in the name of "renewal" (as if things were renewed by being demolished). Varacalli writes:

> In the wake of the Second Vatican Council many of the various Catholic professional associations fell victim either to a "secularization from without," that is, dissolved as specifically "Catholic" organizations or a "secularization from within," that is, internally transformed into shells of their once authentically Catholic selves while still formally keeping the Catholic label. . . . The requirements of "ecumenism," "academic freedom," "critical thinking," and "individual conscience" were used to make the case that distinctive Catholic

academic perspectives and separate (but, again, not isolated) Catholic professional associations were provincial at best or contradictory at worst. . . . Rather than dialoguing with their secular counterparts, many influential post-Vatican II Catholics capitulated to their mindset.

The destruction of the Catholic subculture was one of the major tragedies of the years after the Council. Its outcome was not merely the loss of some organizations and institutions but the de facto disappearance of the Catholic identity of many others and the collapse of the institutional framework required for the transmission of faith.

"Ask any bishop confirming 14-year-olds what the condition of Catholic knowledge is among these young people," says Catholic writer George Weigel, "and you will get one horror story after another." By contrast, he and other Catholics of an earlier generation had the incomparable advantage of growing up in "a more or less intact Catholic culture."

> The schools we went to, the parishes we were in, the people our families associated with — you just absorbed this stuff through your pores. It was not simply a rational process; the behaviors and certain symbolic realities all got absorbed the way you absorb culture. That is what has broken down over the last few years — the transmission belt.

Perhaps it couldn't be helped. Demographic factors like the suburbanization noted above would have had a powerful impact, no matter what. So would changes in catechetical thinking and practice that either shifted the emphasis from transmitting intelligible content to process and experience and "values" or substituted unsound content for what had been sound in the past — or erred in both ways.

But even so, no small part of the breaking down of the Catholic subculture was deliberate, carried out for its own sake. Now, Varacalli says, "Catholic Americans must roll up their sleeves and start the painful process of putting the pieces of their religion back together again."

Politics and Public Life

Nowhere have the consequences of these unhappy developments been more conspicuous than in politics and public life.

Here, as elsewhere, I am obliged to underline the obvious fact that the decline of lay apostolate and the dismantling of the Catholic subculture that had supported the apostolate are hardly the *only* explanations for the disconcerting state of affairs that now exists. But they are part of the explanation — a larger part, perhaps, than is commonly acknowledged by people who have a vested interest in not acknowledging it.

The political situation of American Catholics has changed dramatically in the last several decades. Catholics, at one time reliably Democratic, have become the biggest group of swing voters in America. More and more, their voting patterns have come to mirror those of the electorate as a whole. William B. Prendergast, at the close of his careful historical analysis *The Catholic Voter in American Politics*, published in 1999, ventures this prediction: "The melting pot will in all likelihood continue its work of making Catholics in their political attachments and sentiments less and less distinguishable from the rest of America."

More recent data tend to bear that out in part but at the same time call attention to another, more complex possible scenario.

Shortly before the November, 2000, elections, the Center for Applied Research in the Apostolate, acting at the behest of the Commonweal Foundation and the Faith and Reason Institute, conducted a survey of American Catholics. Along with the finding that only one of them in three now attends Mass weekly or more often, the study showed that Catholics were split down the middle on legalizing assisted suicide, that slightly more regard themselves as pro-choice (49%) than pro-life (45.7%), and that a large majority (62.1%) think abortion should be legal. About 40% admitted that in making political choices they draw on Catholic faith and values only "a little" or (rather more numerous) "not at all."

Looking at these findings, Mary McGrory, longtime political columnist of *The Washington Post* and a Catholic herself, remarked at a news briefing that many American Catholics had evidently been "assimilated into the prevailing attitudes." Indeed they have; but there is nothing new about this. Polls have been telling the same story for years. The newness now, such as it is, is only that the situation appears to be getting worse.

And also more complicated. There is much evidence, strongly reinforced in the election of 2000, that American Catholics, like Americans generally, are now divided into two polarized cultural groups — religious and nonreligious — holding profoundly different views of politics, values, and the meaning of life. The historian Gertrude Himmelfarb, elaborating a view held by many other cultural observers, calls the present-day United States a nation of "two cultures," with all that implies for social and political conflict.

And Catholics? Very large numbers of them now belong to each of the two cultures. On the whole, their attitudes and political behaviors tend to reflect those of Catholic political leadership. The Ethics and Public Policy Center's former president, Elliott Abrams, expresses wonderment at the fact that "most of the prominent national politicians who are Catholics seem in no way to be Catholic. The fact that they are Catholic seems to have no impact on their public careers." Some Catholics wonder about that, too, although they have grown more or less accustomed to the situation.

While it would be a gross oversimplification to put all the responsibility for this state of affairs on just one or two individuals, there is no ignoring the role played by John F. Kennedy in helping to bring it about. Kennedy's election as president in 1960 often is cited as the political coming-of-age of American Catholics. No doubt it was. But it came at a high price, first paid in Houston, Texas, in the midst of the presidential campaign and since then paid over and over again by other Catholic politicians who have followed Kennedy.

The candidate had gone to Houston during the campaign to deliver a speech crafted with the express aim of putting to rest non-Catholic fears about the prospect of having a Catholic chief executive. Delivered to an audience of Protestant ministers, it was a remarkable affair that went a long way to getting him elected. In part he said:

> I believe in an America where the separation of church and state is absolute — where no Catholic prelate would tell the president (should he be a Catholic) how to act and no Protestant minister would tell his parishioners for whom to vote — where no church or church school is granted any public funds or political preference . . . where no public official either requests or accepts instructions on public policy from the Pope, the National Council of Churches or any other ecclesiastical source

— where no religious body seeks to impose its will directly or indirectly upon the general populace or the public acts of its officials.

In case this wasn't enough, Kennedy added:

Whatever issue may come before me as President . . . on birth control, divorce, censorship, gambling, or any other subject — I will make my decision in accordance with . . . what my conscience tells me to be in the national interest, and without regard to outside religious pressure or dictate. And no power or threat of punishment could cause me to do otherwise.

Here Kennedy was setting up straw men in order to knock them down. Much that he so boldly disavowed and pledged to resist assumed the existence of a church-state relationship that had not existed in the West for seven centuries, if ever.

Arguably, Kennedy had to engage in this strange performance if he was to deal successfully with the sort of suspicions he faced in Houston. But he went too far. By declaring that as a Catholic president he would resist pressures that no leader of his Church would have dreamed of trying to place on him, he pandered to bigotry.

Robert P. George, a professor of jurisprudence at Princeton, and William L. Saunders, a senior fellow at the Family Research Council, correctly point out that Kennedy implicitly embraced "the enduring, popular misconception that the Catholic Church seeks to impose her views on (rather than reason with) Americans and declared his independence from any such interference with his conscience, which was itself apparently free to disregard Church teachings. He gave no positive account of how his Catholic faith would help make him a good president; rather, he accepted the view that religion should be separated from public life."

Twenty-four years later, the process that John Kennedy had begun in Houston was carried further by another prominent Catholic politician, Mario Cuomo, governor of New York and at the time widely considered a likely contender for the presidency.

Cuomo's problem was abortion. He wanted it known that, as a Catholic, he "personally" opposed the practice but that, as an officeholder, he would not attempt to translate that position into public policy. He also wished to make the case that this personal-public dichotomy — putting religion in a box and keeping it there — was entirely legitimate for a Catholic in public life.

The governor's tactic, in a speech delivered on September 13, 1984, at the University of Notre Dame, was to wrap himself in the seamless garment of life. "According to Cuomo," George and Saunders explain, "what made a politician truly pro-life and truly someone prepared to act in the spirit of the Catholic teaching was not his opposition to abortion or its public funding. . . . It was, rather, the politician's stance on the whole range of sanctity and quality of life issues. And here, he implied, liberal Democrats, such as himself, who shared the bishops' stated positions on capital punishment, welfare, housing, taxation, defense spending, and international human rights policy had records far superior to those of pro-life conservatives."

George and Saunders call Cuomo's Notre Dame speech a "virtual playbook for pro-abortion Catholic politicians" that taught them how to be "pro-life and pro-choice" at the same time and how to finesse the abortion issue with Catholic voters who might otherwise object.

Today, many American Catholics share the views expressed by Kennedy and Cuomo. As Abrams remarks, "most of the prominent national politicians who are Catholics seem in no way to be Catholic." The same might be said of a substantial body of Catholic voters. We have come a long way from the time when John LaFarge could confidently say Catholics built a bulwark against social evil on the foundation of "the ethical heritage that we enjoy as Catholics through our Church." Some still do that, of course, but many do not; and some of the latter apparently see no reason even to try.

Apostolate Abandoned

I do not want to be misunderstood as claiming too much. Here is another disclaimer.

I neither say nor suggest that abandoning the lay apostolate was the entire cause of the situation described here — the repudiation and dismantling of the Catholic subculture, the assimilation of American Catholics into a secular culture increasingly hostile to their religious tradition, widespread Catholic acceptance of a dichotomy, or split, between religion and public life. Other factors of a sociological and ecclesial nature did their part. My only point is that dropping the idea of lay apostolate fit hand-in-glove with those other factors, just as recapturing it must be part of undoing the harm.

If the Church, renewed by Vatican Council II, had become the culture-forming agent in America that it was poised to become in the 1950s; *if* the Catholic subculture had been similarly renewed and updated, instead of being dismantled; *if* the ideal of lay apostolate in service to the world had continued to burn in zealous Catholic hearts after the Council; *if* the split between faith and life had not gotten a false semblance of legitimacy in the eyes of so many American Catholics from the words and deeds of Catholic public figures and opinion leaders — *if* all these things (and many more besides) somehow were so, the state of the Church and the nation today would be a great deal better than it is. But this is not what happened.

The abandoning of lay apostolate and of the organizations and movements that promoted it was central to the "dangerous and potentially catastrophic" undertaking of which Charles Morris speaks — the project, that is, of cutting the link between the Catholic religion and a living Catholic subculture. Many lay groups were allowed, even encouraged, to wither. Many schools and other institutions became markedly less Catholic in fact, while nevertheless retaining the name. Catholics focused less and less on changing the world, and more and more on issues and controversies in the Church. This was the climate in which lay ministry blossomed and grew.

The 1987 international Synod of Bishops dealt with the role of the laity in the Church and the world. At that time I worked for the national conference of the Catholic bishops of the United States. Months before the assembly in Rome, I was assigned to pull together replies from a number of American dioceses to a Vatican questionnaire inquiring about the state of the laity.

One question was whether Vatican Council II's teaching about laypeople had been "welcomed, understood, and properly presented." Based on diocesan replies, the answer was in part:

> While the number of lay people actively involved in some aspect of the Church's work has increased greatly since Vatican II, they constitute a small minority among the

total number of laity. . . . Lay participation is commonly understood as meaning involvement only in programs and activities of the Church. Few lay people understand or are committed to the apostolate in the secular world.

Another question inquired about "positive fruits" of the Council while asking what "new problems" laypeople had to face in regard to their vocation and mission. The answer was:

While lay participation in ministries and church-related activities has grown, there has been no corresponding increase in lay commitment to evangelization and the renewal of the temporal order. Nothing comparable to the Catholic Action of the 1940s and 1950s has emerged . . . although several respondents suggested that the pro-life movement has this potential.

A third question asked how "consciousness of the necessity and irreplaceability of the pastoral mission of the laity [had] matured." The reply:

Opinions differ. . . . One diocese, striking a middle ground, offered this comment: "There has been a remarkable expansion of lay ministry, primarily at the parish level. . . . This development can be traced directly to the Second Vatican Council. . . . Unfortunately, this has also hindered the full and widespread development of the conciliar teaching on the mission of the laity in the world. . . . The Church does not often highlight and affirm the gifts and responsibilities of the laity to transform the social order."

To be sure, Pope John Paul II did indeed "highlight and affirm" these gifts and responsibilities in *Christifideles Laici*, the document he published after the 1987 Synod. Some others have done the same. But there is no evidence that the situation on the whole has changed for the better. It may have gotten worse.

Apostolate Resisted

It is said that when the subject of lay apostolate is raised with some Catholics today, they react with suspicion and resistance. Partly that may be due to ignorance — the very term "lay apostolate" is unfamiliar to many people — and partly to the lingering notion that "lay apostolate" continues to mean what it so often meant in the days of Catholic Action, namely, a form of lay activity authorized and controlled by clerics. (Vatican II acknowledged the continued validity of the Catholic Action model, but it also made it clear that baptism and confirmation give laypeople a right and obligation to take part in the mission of the Church through their self-initiated, independent apostolic activity in the secular world.)

Ignorance aside, though, I can think of several other reasons for this antipathy to lay apostolate.

First, apostolate is difficult and sometimes even risky. An apostolic woman or man risks being regarded as a prude, a goody-goody, or part of the Christian Right. But along with being embarrassing, it can be dangerous. A doctor who refuses on ethical grounds to perform or refer for immoral procedures may hurt his practice, especially if he or she is in a field like ob-gyn. A similar problem can arise for a lawyer who won't take certain cases or a freelance writer or public relations or advertising consultant who turns down certain assignments or clients. And so on for other professions and kinds of work. Behavior like this can cost a person money, prestige, promotions. It can even cost a job.

Some years ago a friend of mine was finishing up his Ph.D. at a world-class university. He had written his dissertation under the guidance of a renowned scholar and done extremely well. He had every reason to think he would have no trouble getting a teaching job at a quality school.

That seemed on its way to happening after he had a friendly interview at a large secular university in the Midwest. So friendly was it, in fact, that the department chairman volunteered to drive him to the airport for the flight home.

Arriving early, they went to the coffee shop. Over coffee, the department chairman got down to cases. Alluding to my friend's Catholicism, he said, "You don't really believe all that stuff, do you?"

"Bet your life I do."

"Then," said the chairman (rather sadly, it may be), "I'm afraid there's no place for you here."

And there wasn't.

A second reason for the resistance to lay apostolate is alienation, especially anticlericalism. Alienated Catholics typically say, "They can't tell me what to do" — where *they* means the pope, bishops, and priests. To some extent, that is a reaction against the clerical authority of the past and its sometimes heavy-handed exercise, which was, or in hindsight at least now appears to have been, the Achilles' heel of Catholic Action. Today, we have swung to the other extreme.

Sometimes one even comes across Catholics hostile to the very idea that the Church should do or say anything regarding the great public issues of the day. Persuaded, it seems, by the rhetoric of absolute separation of church and state, these people have accepted the idea of a divorce between religion and the political order. On one level, of course, this reflects the influence of a secularist interpretation of the

Religion Clauses of the Constitution's First Amendment that the Founding Fathers would not recognize. On a deeper level, one suspects, it reflects Catholic anticlericalism and alienation.

A third reason is the common idea that lay ministry is the best expression of the lay vocation, the best form of lay participation in the mission of the Church. And why shouldn't people think that? By now they have been told it often enough.

They have been told it in deeds — the emphasis on ministry and neglect of apostolate in official circles for many years. And they have been told it in so many words — for example, when someone like Father Thomas O'Meara, O.P., says (in his influential *Theology of Ministry*) that the very term "apostolate of the laity" expresses the "deficiencies" of earlier initiatives like Catholic Action and must give way to the language and behaviors associated with "ministry." This message has had an impact on not a few Catholics, lay as well as clerical.

Finally, the resistance to lay apostolate may in part reflect a suspicion that talk about the laity's role in the secular world is a ploy by clerics to keep laypeople out of positions of authority in the Church and retain control of the levers of power for themselves. Very likely such an attitude does linger on in some places; yet these days I doubt that it is a conscious motive of many priests and bishops.

To the extent that it is a real problem, nevertheless, it should be corrected. Consistent with that, I shall say something below (in the appendix of this book) about shared responsibility in the Church, and especially about the need to create appropriate structures for it. Here I merely wish to point out that, even if some such problem as this exists, that is no reason for rejecting the idea of lay apostolate.

There is a strong case to be made for lay ministry. But it should be made on its merits, not at the expense of apostolate. In making the case for lay ministry, furthermore, some confusions and problems associated with it need to be honestly faced. Let us turn now to both things — the case for ministry and some associated problems.

FOUR

'Mass Is Downstairs'

Back in 1997 the Vatican published a document whose ponderous title, *Instruction on Certain Questions Regarding the Collaboration of the Non-Ordained Faithful in the Sacred Ministry of Priests*, was enough by itself to guarantee that few American Catholics would read it. Most, in fact, have no idea it exists. But the *Instruction* deserves attention.

For one thing, it was significant enough that top officials of no fewer than eight Vatican agencies signed it, including the heads of the Congregation for the Doctrine of the Faith, the Congregation for Bishops, the Congregation for the Clergy, and the Pontifical Council for the Laity. Moreover, at the same time it was being generally ignored, it also was received with hostility and biting criticism by many of those who did take note of it, a good sign that, for better or worse, it said something important.

The critics complained that the *Instruction* was an attempt by the Vatican to slam the lid on lay ministry, which had been flourishing up to that time. If there were any real problems with ministries, it was said, they were to be found in Europe, where lay pastoral associates in some places were performing functions reserved to priests. No such abuses existed in the United States, the critics maintained; so here the *Instruction* could and should be ignored.

Others weren't so sure about that.

In a paper for a colloquium called "Toward a Theology of Ecclesial Lay Ministry," sponsored by the U.S. bishops' conference, Bishop Howard J. Hubbard of Albany, New York, suggested the need for concrete measures ("clear diocesan guidelines and nomenclature, ministerial criteria, hiring protocol, evaluation procedures, and grievance mechanisms") to preserve the distinctions underlined in the Vatican document, guard against a "congregational mentality," and strengthen the relationship between lay ministers and their dioceses. All these are matters, remarked Bishop Hubbard (in whose diocese lay ministry has been actively promoted), "which our own experience in Albany and the observations of others raise as a potentially serious concern."

At this point, though, it might be a good idea to take a look at what *Instruction on Certain Questions Regarding the Collaboration of the Non-Ordained Faithful in the Sacred Ministry of Priests* actually says.

Although misrepresented in some quarters as a slap at the laity, the document is really not that. Undoubtedly it is sparing in its praise of lay ministry — possibly *too* sparing, in fact — but that can be understood in light of its purpose.

As the title suggests, this is an attempt to spell out how laypeople can collaborate in the ministry of priests, without confusing or collapsing the distinction between clerics and laity. "It is necessary that all who are in any way involved in this collaboration exercise particular care to safeguard the nature and mission of sacred ministry and the vocation and secular character of the lay faithful," the *Instruction* says.

The document speaks of the "very positive" progress achieved by priest-laity collaboration and pays tribute to its good results. Even so, it says, "certain practices have often been developed which have had very serious negative consequences." This seems all too likely, considering the state of affairs described by the American theologian Avery Dulles, S.J. (named a cardinal on February 21, 2001): Many Catholic intellectuals in America and Western Europe today "either reject the concept of ministerial priesthood or redefine it in ways that make it scarcely distinguishable from the concept of ministry in Protestant Congregationalism."

Hence the need for clear distinctions. The *Instruction* stresses the fundamental distinction pointed out by Vatican II: The priesthood of the faithful (in which all baptized persons share) and the ministerial priesthood (which belongs only to ordained priests) "differ essentially and not only in degree" (*Lumen Gentium*, 10). Laypeople can cooperate with priests in some (but not all) functions of the latter if they are authorized to do so; but, as Pope John Paul has said, this does not "make pastors of the lay faithful," and the ordained priesthood remains "absolutely irreplaceable."

The *Instruction* insists on the use of "appropriate terminology" in order to avoid confusion. "It must be admitted that the language [of ministry] becomes doubtful, confused, and hence not helpful," it says. This is an observation whose truth surely must be apparent to anyone who has had to wrestle with these terminological matters for himself.

The document declares it "unlawful" for laypeople to assume titles like "pastor," "chaplain," "coordinator," "moderator," and the like, which can seem to equate their role with the role of a priest. It lays down restrictions on things like preaching and pastoral work (the collaboration of laypeople in pastoral ministry is said to be appropriate where there is a shortage of priests, but "not for reasons of convenience or ambiguous 'advancement of the laity' "), liturgical services, and sacramental functions. "The object of this document," it concludes, "is to outline specific directives to ensure the effective collaboration of the non-ordained faithful . . . while safeguarding the integrity of the pastoral ministry of priests."

Except in the eyes of persons with a chip-on-the-shoulder attitude toward anything from Rome, it would be hard to say what is objectionable about that. Even in the United States, it seems, the matters the *Instruction* treats already are real issues and may become matters of even more concern in the future.

How that could happen was suggested in a paper by Bishop Kenneth E. Untener of Saginaw, Michigan, appearing in a book published in 1994, three years before the Vatican document. There he spoke of what had happened in his diocese, where "word and communion" services conducted by non-ordained persons had been introduced in some parishes in response to the shortage of priests.

> The people call it Mass. The pastoral administrators try till they are blue in the face to say that this is not Mass. Sister Nancy, who has been in one parish seven years, told me she has given up fighting it. In the wintertime, during the week, if it was really cold, they would sometimes have the service downstairs in the basement, which is easier to heat for a small group. For seven years, when people used to say, "Sister Nancy, is the Mass upstairs or downstairs?" she would say, "It is not a Mass, it is a communion service." She tells me, "Know what I say now? 'Mass is downstairs.' "

Making distinctions obviously isn't going to be the total solution to a problem like that; but there will be no solution at all unless the distinctions get made.

It is likely that the confusion depicted in Bishop Untener's anecdote will get worse as the priest shortage spreads. The number of American priests has been dropping for three decades, from more than 59,000 in 1970 to 46,000 in 2000 (about 30,500 diocesan priests and some 15,000 religious). During these years, the percentage of active diocesan priests between the ages of 25 and 34 declined by half, to about 5%, while the percentage over 55 increased 50% (to about 59% of the total, including a considerable number older than 75). By 2000, the average age of diocesan priests in active ministry in the U.S. was 59; for religious priests, it was 63.

Meanwhile seminary enrollments have fallen sharply, from slightly over 8,000 students in theologates in 1967-1968 (5,000 diocesan, 3,000 religious) to fewer than 4,000 by 2000 (just over 3,000 diocesan, well under 1,000 religious). There was a corresponding drop in ordinations. In 1960, about 500 U.S. parishes were without a resident pastor; 40 years later it was about 2,500 — 13% of the total — although with significant variations from one region of the country to another. According to a projection, by the year 2010 there will be a little over 15,000 active diocesan priests in the U.S.; there were about 19,500 parishes in 2000.

Obviously others besides priests will have to step in — they are doing so already in fact — to help fill the gap. To some extent, the 12,000 permanent deacons in the U.S. are playing this role. So, increasingly, are lay ministers, both volunteer and professional. We should be glad and grateful that they are.

Lay Ministers and LEMs

At a colloquium on lay ministry sponsored in 1997 by the U.S. bishops' conference, Father Thomas O'Meara, O.P., called the form of lay ministry that has grown up since Vatican

Council II "qualitatively different" from the lay movements and organizations — things like third orders and confraternities, Catholic Action, the Vincent de Paul and Holy Name Societies, and others — that preceded it.

Earlier expressions of lay activism, he said, took for granted the distinction between the realms of the "sacral" and "sacred." (Since in most people's vocabularies "sacral" and "sacred" mean pretty much the same thing, one can only suppose he meant "religious" and "secular.") In so doing, they failed to "pass beyond witness and material assistance into the essential ministries of the Church." Then came the revolution.

> In the 1970s, parishioners' activities underwent a pneumatic metamorphosis as men and women (and permanent deacons) became active in liturgical ministries during and outside of Mass as well as in services of education, liturgy, peace and justice, music, and ministry to the sick and dying. If we focus on the basic place of ministry — the parish, from 1965 to 1975 — parishes changed in terms of which ministries were done and in terms of who did them. The parish was no longer a place of rapid Masses and group baptisms in Latin with an occasional picnic or parish dance. The liturgy, including deacons, lectors, cantors, and communion bearers, illustrates the expansion of the ministry outside of Sunday morning in church.

There are several things to note about this passage. One is that Father O'Meara's comments are rather seriously confused. Where, after all, are all those liturgies involving deacons, lectors, cantors, and eucharistic ministers mainly taking place except on "Sunday morning in church"? Does the author mean that lay ministry extends to more than the Sunday liturgy? This is so self-evidently the case that it hardly needs saying. Does he therefore mean to make some other point? It is impossible to tell.

Another difficulty is the patronizing caricature here substituted for the complex reality of the not-so-distant Catholic past. American Catholics who grew up in reasonably healthy parishes in the 1940s and 1950s did not experience them merely as places that offered "rapid Masses and group baptisms in Latin with an occasional picnic or parish dance." Parish life was far richer and more exciting than that.

In parishes of that era, many people participated in Mass and/or devotions on weekdays and regularly received the sacrament of Penance. In general, the music was better then than now, even though popular hymns undoubtedly were sentimental (but so are many of the popular hymns that have replaced them today), and choir music often was more of a performance than it was sound liturgy (that remains the case).

Parishes of that day had their limitations, to be sure, but so do parishes now. In many cases, these latter include vast size and impersonality, tensions of various sorts (racial, ethnic, generational, ideological — conservatives versus liberals, liturgical traditionalists versus the folk group, etc.), poor or nonexistent catechesis for many age groups, the known presence within the parish borders of a substantial number of alienated, nonpracticing Catholics whom no one thinks of inviting to church, and quite a bit else. It serves no useful purpose to trash the parishes of the past in order to idealize today's parish life.

All that aside, however, Father O'Meara does provide a fairly typical overview of the expansion of lay ministry in the Church in the United States in the last four decades. A momentous change has indeed taken place. And, for the most part, this change is welcome.

But it is a curious feature of the literature on lay ministry that it tends to give comparatively little attention to the vast body of *volunteer* lay ministers operating in parishes and other Church settings today, even while devoting a great deal of attention to the far smaller number of *professional, salaried* "lay ecclesial ministers." That may be because most of what is written about lay ministry is produced by people, both clerical and lay, who themselves are part of the Church's professional class.

It is important to keep the distinctions here clearly in view. The difference between volunteer lay ministers and professional, salaried lay ecclesial ministers was underlined by Cardinal Roger Mahony of Los Angeles in a pastoral letter on ministry issued in April of 2000.

First he made the important point that most laypersons are "called to transform the world by living out their baptismal vocations, being and becoming the body of Christ in the world, advancing the kingdom of God amid the pressing demands of marriage, family, school and workplace." Then he noted ways in which laypeople perform ministerial functions on a volunteer basis in the Church — "through the proclamation of the word in word and in deed, through the liturgical ministries of lector, musician or eucharistic minister, through the many other ministries which serve to animate the community gathered for prayer."

Only then did he speak of a third group:

> In our own day . . . some laypersons are called to "lay ecclesial ministry," a vocation of full-time church service in response to the needs of each local community. This must be distinguished from the vocation of all the baptized to advance the reign of God through their commitments to marriage and family, workplace and social

responsibility. It must also be distinguished from the many other lay ministries. . . . Within the context of the common call to service which is given to all the baptized, *lay ecclesial ministry* refers to professionally trained or otherwise properly prepared women and men, including vowed religious, who are in positions of service and leadership in the Church.

While calling lay ecclesial ministry "a unique vocation," Cardinal Mahony nevertheless notes that the name does not refer to only one kind of activity or one role. In fact, lay ecclesial ministers hold jobs like pastoral associate, parish business manager, director of religious education, catechist, director of the RCIA (Rite of Christian Initiation of Adults) program, youth/young adult minister, and liturgical coordinator; often, the same individual wears more than one of these hats.

The cardinal goes on to say that the term "lay ecclesial ministry" refers to ministry that is exercised in a "stable, public, recognized and authorized" manner. "This is Church ministry in the strict and formal sense," he declares.

Technically speaking, though, that is not correct. "Ministry" in a "strict and formal sense" pertains properly to persons who are ordained; their sacramental configuration to Christ in Holy Orders makes it possible for them to minister in his person — to act *in persona Christi capitis*, as the old expression has it, in the Eucharist and the sacrament of Penance performing the acts of Christ himself as his proxies.

Laypeople, as we saw earlier, participate analogically in ministry. And since lay ecclesial ministers are not ordained, their ministry is ministry in an analogical sense, not in its proper sense. This does not make it any less worthwhile. But it is important to insist on the point, in order to avoid a kind of de facto relativizing of ordained ministry — as if there were one fundamental thing called "ministry," of which ordained and non-ordained ministries are accidentally different but essentially alike expressions: rather in the way that, although a baseball team has a second baseman, a shortstop, a center fielder, and soon, all of them nevertheless are the same thing at bottom — ballplayers.

Profiling Lay Ministry

There is a profile of lay ministry — mainly, lay ecclesial ministry — in a fact sheet prepared by the Secretariat for Family, Laity, Women, and Youth of the U.S. bishops' conference. Based on information drawn from *Parishes and Parish Ministers: A Study of Parish Lay Ministers*, by Monsignor Philip J. Murnion and David DeLambo (New York: National Pastoral Life Center, 1999), it provides these nuggets of information.

- As of 1997, there were 29,146 parish lay ministers in the United States who were paid for at least 20 hours' work a week. This represented a 35% increase in the paid lay ministry work force since 1992.
- In that same year 63% of the parishes in the U.S. had lay parish ministers. The figure was 54% five years earlier.
- Of the "lay" parish ministers in 1997, 29% were religious sisters or brothers; they made up 42% of this group in 1992. The change evidently reflects a declining number of religious and a rising number of parish ministers.
- In 1997, 82% of the lay parish ministers were women.
- In 1997, 6.4% of lay parish ministers were Hispanic, African American, Asian American, or Native Ameri-

can. In the case of Hispanics especially, that figure was far below their present numbers in the overall Catholic population — 30%, perhaps more, depending on how one counts the number of Hispanic Catholics. In that year, 17% of the Catholic parishes in the country celebrated at least one Mass in Spanish, but only 4.4% of parish lay ministers were Hispanics.

- Eight out of 10 lay parish ministers in 1997 had a college education; 53.5% had a master's degree or better.
- One-fourth of the religious sisters and brothers and 55.3% of the laypeople working as parish ministers said the time might come when they no longer could afford financially to work for the Church. About one-third said their present salaries were not adequate to their needs, appropriate to the work they did and the expertise it required, or competitive with salaries paid for other, comparable jobs. Many nevertheless acknowledged that their parishes couldn't afford more.
- More than 90% agreed or agreed strongly with these statements: "Ministry has been affirming to me," "I am adequately able to develop and use my talents in my present position," "My superiors in the parish are satisfied with my performance as a minister," and "My work is recognized and affirmed by the parishioners I serve." This apparently rather one-sided emphasis on personal gratification in the case of people committed to serving others may seem a bit odd; but, be that as it may, the responses do indicate a high degree of job satisfaction among these parish ministers.

The fact sheet also included a few statistics on other groups besides parish lay ministers.

- In the 1999-2000 school year, according to the National Catholic Educational Association, 93% (146,123) of the teachers and principals in Catholic elementary and secondary schools in the United States were laypeople, while 7% (11,011) were priests, religious sisters, and brothers. This was the reverse of the situation in 1920, when the vast majority of teachers and administrators were religious and priests, and just a handful of laypeople held such jobs.

(It was unusual, by the way, for the fact sheet even to mention lay personnel in Catholic schools, since official lay ministry literature rarely takes note of them. The people who write about lay ministry appear mainly interested in lay ecclesial ministers — persons engaged in salaried pastoral work in parishes and other Church settings — and exhibit surprisingly little interest in Catholic schoolteachers and lay volunteers. It is not entirely clear why this is so, since, among other things, the teachers and volunteers are far more numerous than lay ecclesial ministers. If I had to make a guess, nevertheless, I would say this was the clericalist mentality at work: Lay ecclesial ministers tend to do things that, at one time, were done almost exclusively by clerics; and as salaried full-time professionals, often working in rectories and pastoral centers, they are readily accepted as adjunct members of the clerical club. There is nothing premeditated or surprising about all this, but it is worth bearing in mind when trying to understand what is really going on.)

- In 1997, about 2,730 laypeople — "including vowed religious" — were certified members of the National Association of Catholic Chaplains. Most served in hospitals, nursing and retirement homes, hospices, mental hospitals, and rehabilitation centers, but a growing number were in parishes.
- The American Catholic Correctional Chaplains Association in 1997 had 230 members, 55% of them lay, serving in federal, state, county, and municipal prisons. In that year, too, the 35 members of the National Catholic Conference for Seafarers, an association of seaport chaplains, included 9 laywomen and laymen, and the Catholic Campus Ministry Association had 900 lay members.

The Case for Lay Ministry

As is clear from these figures, something significant is happening in the area of lay ministry. Not only is lay ministry already contributing to Catholic life, but it also holds out much hope for the future. Pope John Paul II stressed the positive in his apostolic letter closing the Year 2000 Jubilee when he called on the Church of the third millennium to "make room for all the gifts of the Spirit."

> The Church of the third millennium will need to encourage all the baptized and confirmed to be aware of their active responsibility in the Church's life. Together with the ordained ministry, other ministries, whether formally instituted or simply recognized, can flourish for the good of the whole community, sustaining it in all its many needs: from catechesis to liturgy, from the

education of the young to the widest array of charitable works.

Speaking from a U.S. perspective, Albany's Bishop Howard Hubbard reports that, along with doing much good work themselves, lay ministers, "both salaried and volunteer," also are effective in "recruiting, supporting, and affirming" other laypeople for ministerial roles.

For example, many of the laity who have completed our Formation for Ministry program have enabled others to serve as parish retreat leaders or leaders of small faith sharing and Scripture study groups; as members of bereavement, hospitality, youth, young adult and social action committees; as participants on AIDS care teams or on retreat teams for those in local jails and state prisons or for those with developmental disabilities; and as people willing to share with the wider community their professional expertise in areas such as counseling of the unemployed, assisting immigrants with legal problems and language skills, and offering medical and nursing care in parish or school-based health programs.

Although some of these functions represent the institutionalization as "ministries" of things that ought naturally to be happening in parishes anyway (and that quite possibly did happen, spontaneously and naturally, in earlier times, when American Catholic parishes often were more close-knit human communities than most are now), they nevertheless are praiseworthy things for people to be doing. Even so, there are some questions about lay ministry that need to be asked and answered — not to discourage its continued growth but to make sure it grows well.

Speaking at the bishops' colloquium mentioned earlier, Bishop Hubbard said experience in Albany led to the conclusion "that the development of lay ministry — mostly salaried and at the parish level — requires a more careful assessment of what is happening both with regard to the activities being performed and the nomenclature being employed." The aim, he explained, should be "greater clarity and uniformity throughout the diocese with regard to the terminology being utilized, the expected competencies required, and the relationship of these ministers to the local church." Herewith some preliminary thoughts regarding the assessment he suggests.

There are several obvious arguments in favor of lay ministry. One, already mentioned, is the need for the laity (and permanent deacons and religious) to take up the slack as the priest shortage deepens. Laypeople, religious, and deacons cannot do everything priests can do, especially celebrate Mass and hear confessions; but there is a great deal that they *can* do — administer parishes, conduct communion services and bring communion to the house-bound and hospitalized, teach catechism, do counseling, and a lot else. Let us be glad they can.

Cardinal Mahony describes mythical "St. Leo's Parish" where a priest-pastor and a pastoral team work together to provide a number of services in response to people's needs.

> The pastor, pastoral associate, deacon and other members of the parish staff gather on Monday evenings with each of the following groups in rotation: catechists, teachers, leaders of small groups and animators of various ministries and initiatives within the parish. Their focus is less on programs and organizations and more on communities of mission and ministry: feeding the

poor of the parish and beyond, visiting those shut-in, preparing couples for marriage, working in RCIA teams to assure readiness for sacramental initiation into the Church and organizing circles of catechists devoted to the religious education of children, teens and adults. All are invited to look at their own lives and the life of St. Leo's Parish in light of the Sunday readings, discerning how the word is calling for their own transformation, for the transformation of the whole Church and the wider world.

Probably few priests and laypeople currently are ready for such intense, disciplined, and in-depth continuing collaboration. But, spurred on by simple necessity, the day may be coming when it, or at least something approaching it, will be a reality in some parishes or even many.

The priest shortage is hardly something to be welcomed, but it need not mean all is lost for the Church in the United States. Lay ministry is one ray of hope in this picture. But at the same time that we recognize it and welcome it as such, we need also to be aware that in parishes functioning as parishes should, not just a small number of paid staff and volunteers but *everyone* (except, of course, those prevented by age, health, family duties, or job) would be working together with their pastors to supply the mutual service and forms of help that we lately have taken to calling "ministries."

Nevertheless, as matters stand, there certainly is something admirable about the spirit of lay ministers who persevere in efforts to serve despite the frustrations and disappointments many of them undoubtedly face.

Mercy Sister Amy Hoey, the staff person for lay ecclesial ministry at the U.S. bishops' conference, speaks of "the gap between the 'holy hill' of the seminary or theological school" — where many lay ecclesial ministers get their training these days — "and the gritty world of the real parish." In that gritty world, she points out, "after months of careful planning and preparation," six people may show up for an evening program in a parish; it is a world, too, where women in diocesan leadership positions not infrequently have the experience of being "invisible" in decision-making sessions or simply in informal conversations.

The involvement of non-ordained persons in ecclesial ministries is, however, more than just an interim response to a shortage of priests. It is a good thing in itself — for laypeople, an expression of their role in the Church. To some extent, at least, it marks the recovery of an earlier view of the laity that was largely lost sight of during centuries of clericalist thinking.

"Ministry does not emanate from scarcity, right, or even personal ability," says Cardinal Francis George, O.M.I., of Chicago, summing up the teaching of the Magisterium on this subject. Even the much-maligned *Instruction on Certain Questions Regarding the Collaboration of the Non-Ordained Faithful in the Sacred Ministry of Priests* remarks that when laypeople collaborate in the ministry of the Church's pastors, the resulting relationship is "not one merely of assistance but of mutual enrichment of the common Christian vocation."

The lay ministers themselves see it that way. Zeni Fox, a writer on the subject, reports on a survey:

> Ecclesial ministers do not think that the primary reason they are employed is because of a shortage of priests or of women religious. Those reasons were ranked third and fourth. The first two reasons, by a strong margin, were that the community recognizes the need for the

areas of specialization for which they are trained and that a variety of gifts are given to various members of the community. Perhaps the first reason is shaped by the increasing specialization found in the larger culture, and the second by a memory of the variety of gifts and ministries found in the New Testament communities.

It is important to view lay ministry in vocational terms. Like any other form of participation in the mission of the Church, including lay apostolate, ministry should not be understood as just a job, a task, a way of "helping out" — a set of activities for which people can be recruited and trained more or less indiscriminately; instead lay ministry should be seen as an element of the personal vocations of the lay ministers, a matter for discernment more than for recruitment. This is no less true of volunteer lay ministers than it is of full-time salaried persons.

From that perspective, one can only conclude that a writer who suggests that lay ecclesial ministry is "a response to a genuine call from God" but volunteer lay ministry is not, is seriously missing the point. And the point is that laypersons engaged in volunteer lay ministry should view it as part of their personal vocations, while people who write and speak about lay ministry should help them do that, not pooh-pooh the idea. Yet this pejorative notion — that lay ecclesial ministry is a real vocation, volunteer lay ministry is not — lies just below the surface of much of the writing about ministry. There is a distinction between the two, of course, but it is more sociological than ecclesial; it is simply not the case that one is "vocation" and the other is not.

Here, too, clericalism is at work. This reluctance to admit that laypeople in volunteer ministries are responding to authentic vocations is part of the residue of clericalist thinking. Previously it was supposed that the only real vocations were callings to the priesthood and religious life. Now the clericalist mentality is prepared to admit lay ecclesial ministry (but not volunteer ministry) to the charmed circle. Is that because the full-time salaried ministers are, or are on the way to becoming, clericalized, while the lay volunteers generally aren't?

Whatever the reason, it would be a good idea to drop this clericalist prejudice once and for all. There should be forthright recognition that laypeople who, after a process of conscientious discernment, find themselves called to ministry, whether on a volunteer or full-time basis, are discerning an important element of their personal vocations — subject, of course, to confirmation by a pastor or other ecclesial authority able to accept their services and employ them. That is something to celebrate, not talk down.

Some Problems . . .

No one looking seriously at lay ministries in American Catholicism can help noticing certain problems. There should be no surprise about that. After all, both the idea and practice of lay ministry are quite new in modern times, and some mistakes and confusion inevitably have occurred. It is in everyone's best interests to take an honest look at these miscues.

One source of possible confusion from the priest's perspective is noted by Cardinal Mahony: "Since some of what the priest does is becoming more and more interchangeable with what the laypeople do, this may result in an identity crisis for the ordained minister."

Some of the priest's functions are interchangeable with those of laypeople, but certainly not all: The Eucharist is by far the most notable case. But as Bishop Untener's anecdote about communion services in Saginaw suggests, laypeople regularly exposed to priestless "Masses" may start to suppose they are getting the real thing.

Even among people aware of the difference, I have encountered the attitude that, when all is said and done, it doesn't matter awfully much. A man who had read something I wrote on the subject wrote to say that even though attending a communion service is "not the same as the glory of attending Mass," people at communion services nevertheless do get "both Scripture and sacrament in a regular, formal way." The implication seems to be: "So what's the big deal? Isn't receiving communion what really counts — the 'pay-off' for attending Mass, as it were?" This misses the crucial point that the Mass gives those who participate an opportunity to cooperate directly in Jesus' self-offering and join themselves to him in that sacrifice.

It would be tragic if the spread of communion services conducted by non-ordained ministers to cope with the shortage of priests encouraged some Catholics in a shallow and theologically incorrect view of the eucharistic celebration. Here, after all, is the preeminent act of public worship that, according to the "Constitution on the Sacred Liturgy" of the Second Vatican Council, is "the summit toward which the activity of the Church is directed [and] the fount from which all her power flows" (*Sacrosanctum Concilium*, 10). If people come to imagine that a communion service is, all things considered, a pretty adequate substitute for the Mass, we will be in very bad trouble.

Perhaps it was this sort of concern that not long ago led an anonymous writer in a Catholic periodical to provide a cynic's definition of lay ministry: "The inalienable right of the laity to assume the duties of the clergy in anticipation of the day when the Church is Protestant." That recalled a French definition of Catholic Action back when it was riding high: an attempt to remedy the incompetence (*l'insuffisance*) of the clergy by the impertinence (*la suffisance*) of the laity. Such churchy jokes may or may not strike one as funny, but they do express something of the truth.

There also is reason to be concerned lest lay ministry's spread lend witting or unwitting support to the clericalist idea that, despite what Vatican II said to the contrary, *real* lay participation in the Church's mission takes place in an ecclesiastical setting and involves doing something formerly done only by clerics, instead of taking place out in the secular world and involving the kinds of things laypeople naturally do there. Strenuous efforts will be needed to prevent this way of thinking from arising, or counter it where it already exists. And the problem is only heightened by the rise of full-time lay ecclesial ministry as a Church career, thereby separating a group of salaried specialists even from lay volunteers.

In this context it is disturbing to find a bishop (specifically, Bishop Matthew Clark of Rochester, New York) recommending that "diocesan ministerium" (an expression modeled on "diocesan presbyterium," or body of priests) become a term of art referring to "all those who exercise in the local church an official ecclesial ministry, whether they are ordained or not." In this manner, he explains, "the bishop can more readily form a relationship with lay ecclesial ministers — as he does with presbyters and priests."

This is a well-intentioned suggestion whose practical result would be to separate lay ecclesial ministers from the rest of the laity and treat them like members of the clergy. No less unblushingly clericalist in its implications is Zeni Fox's proposal that the bishops establish a "ritual" designating laypeople as ecclesial ministers: that is to say, a quasi-ordination rite for select laypersons that would set them apart from other laypeople and help them to resemble priests. (Besides their clericalism, such ideas embody the relativizing of ordained ministry mentioned above as an impending problem. On the whole, they tend in the direction of that unfortunate "clericalizing the laity and laicizing the clergy" about which thoughtful observers of Catholic life frequently warn.)

There are some notable examples of clericalist thinking in the media kit for the Jubilee Day for Lay Ministers distributed by the U.S. bishops' conference. One item tells of a permanent deacon who "spent more than 30 years with Fortune 500 companies before coming to work for the church" as human resources director for a diocese; he speaks of the "many talented professionals who 'feel a void in their lives' " and who, "given the right opportunities," would "come to work here [that is, come to work for the Church] in a heartbeat. . . . We have the resources available, and if we develop them well and put everything in place, the Church can in fact be completely successful in this matter."

It goes without saying that much good will underlies such a remark. But does the Church's success really lie in persuading professionals to quit their jobs and come to work in a chancery office or parish? Working for the Church belongs to the vocations of some laywomen and laymen, but the vocations of many others call them to stay right where they are, out in the secular world, doing secular work. They should be encouraged to understand their work as a context and opportunity for apostolate by which they can bring the message of the Gospel to bear upon the evangelization of culture in a way beyond the reach of the clergy. It is well-meaning clericalism, but clericalism nonetheless, to set a premium on recruiting such people for the Church.

Other more or less problematical aspects of full-time lay ecclesial ministry as it currently stands can be seen in some of the numbers cited above. It is nearly all-white (93%) and overwhelmingly female (82% as of 1997), a circumstance that can only add to the growing, widely recognized problem of feminization in the Church. (Perhaps there is a better ethnic and gender balance among the lay ministry volunteers, but numbers are lacking to show whether that is so.)

Yet far and away the biggest problem is that the nearly exclusive emphasis on lay ministry contributes much to the continued neglect of lay apostolate. In some quarters, apostolate is out and ministry is in for today's with-it Catholic laity. What a sad mistake!

The results are particularly visible in regard to lay formation. A Catholic News Service story in early 2001, reporting on new graduate programs for lay ministry in Catholic colleges and universities, quotes a lay ministry official: "Laypeople are flocking to theology schools, and some schools are bursting at the seams." "This is a need that continues to grow," one says. Needless to say, the story cites no academic programs in lay apostolate. Perhaps none are needed. But there is an immense need for *formation* for the apostolate — a need that today goes almost entirely unmet.

Meanwhile, the fact sheet disseminated by the Secretariat for Family, Laity, Women, and Youth of the bishops' conference gives these figures on formation for ministry, drawn from *Catholic Ministry Formation Directory 1999* (Washington: Center for Applied Research in the Apostolate, 1999).

- In 1998-1999, there were 29,137 students enrolled in 279 lay ministry formation programs in the United States, compared with 10,500 students in 206 programs in 1986. Programs existed in 150 dioceses and each of the 50 states and the District of Columbia.
- Women outnumbered men nearly two to one.
- Seventy-one percent of the students were white, 23% Hispanic/Latino, 3% African American, 2% Asian, and 1% Native American. (The comparatively high percentage of Hispanics is a hopeful sign.)
- About 1 student in 4 was younger than 40, over 60% of the students were between the ages of 40 and 60, and 7% were under 30.
- Dioceses or archdioceses sponsored 189 of the formation programs. Colleges and universities sponsored 96 programs, most of them offering degrees, including graduate degrees, and many also offering certificates.
- The graduate degrees most commonly granted are the M.A. in Pastoral Studies or Pastoral Ministry, the M.A. in Religious Education, and the M.A. in Theology or Theological Studies. Nine programs offered doctoral degrees (Ph.D., D.Min., S.T.D.).
- The most common certificates were in catechetics, youth ministry, and liturgy.
- Two hundred twenty-nine programs used only English as the language of instruction, 41 used English and Spanish, and 12 used only Spanish. (This adds up to more than the total of 279 programs reported. No explanation is offered.) Other languages included Portuguese, Navajo, and sign language.

Who pays for the formation of the lay ministers? Often, of course, the aspiring ministers themselves — an expression of commendable commitment on their part. In many cases, though, dioceses and parishes subsidize the training in whole or in part. Not only is nothing comparable done to help people prepare for apostolate, the whole subject of formation for apostolate is, for the most part, simply ignored in most Church settings today.

...And Some Questions

Certain unanswered questions about lay ministry call for a great deal more forthright discussion than they generally have received up to now.

One of these questions concerns women in ministry. A report by the executive committee of the Leadership Conference of Women Religious, whose members are heads of women's religious institutes in the United States, reads in part as follows: "As long as jurisdiction (the power to govern) is tied to ordination, a very limited number of roles with authority will be open to women. The relationship of jurisdiction to ordination creates a glass ceiling for women in the Church. This seems markedly inconsistent with recent pledges made by the Church to involve women in governance and to advance the cause of women."

Governance is a complex canonical issue whose technical ins and outs need not concern us now. It seems probable that most laywomen engaged in ministry have little or no interest in acquiring powers of governance: They minister because they want to help, not because they want to be in charge of something. Very likely this also is the attitude of most religious women in ministry (and also most men).

But the LCWR executive committee's comment nevertheless raises this question: If lay ecclesial ministry puts women in positions where the question of governance arises, and if governance in the Church is tied to ordination, what relationship exists in fact (whether it is recognized and admitted or not) between lay ecclesial ministry for women and women's ordination as priests?

Two possibilities come to mind. One is that lay ecclesial ministry by women is meant as a *substitute* for priestly ordination. The other is that it is intended as an interim stage on the way. (I recall, by the way, a secular journal article some years back in which the president of a major Catholic university in the United States said that was how things stood on his campus at the time: Women there were being pressed forward in liturgical and other roles, in anticipation of the day when they would be ordained.)

Either possibility involves playing with fire on a notably volatile issue. A Catholic News Service story in September, 1999, reported on a Women's Ordination Conference study purporting to show that many women who "feel called to ordination" are engaged in full-time ministry. The finding obviously had to be taken with more than one grain of salt, since this was a study reflecting the views of a self-selected group of participants, carried out by an advocacy group that lobbies for women's ordination as priests. As such, it had no scientific value at all. But it did point to a reality about lay ministry that, even if very limited in scope (and there is no evidence that it is), cannot responsibly be swept under the rug.

There is not much consolation either in Sister Amy Hoey's assurance that people in ministry training programs have "achieved some degree of peace with current [unspecified] church teaching." Better for them and everyone else if they gladly accepted Catholic teaching and looked forward with enthusiasm to the privileged work of sharing it with others. Some do of course; one might wish all did.

Lay ministry is a good thing in itself and increasingly necessary, too. That is true both of the volunteer lay ministry in which so many women and men generously and selflessly take part and of the full-time salaried lay ecclesial ministry in which a much smaller number now are carving out careers in Church work. But before we travel much farther down this path, concerns and questions like the ones noted here must be acknowledged and addressed.

Especially, we need to consider the implications of the fact that lay apostolate has consistently been ignored during the several decades in which lay ministry has enjoyed the ascendancy in official circles. Speaking of the practice of emphasizing ecclesial ministries "almost to the detriment or exclusion" of the apostolate in the secular world, Bishop Hubbard says:

> It is critically important, therefore, that in defining ecclesial lay ministry, we not do so in a way that deemphasizes or detracts from the vital and indispensable role the laity have in the home, on the job, and in the neighborhood, the community, and the marketplace to be about the transformation of society and to make the gospel message real in the family, in social life, in business transactions, and in the world of politics.

He is entirely correct.

FIVE

Ministry *and* Apostolate

A girl e-mailed her grandfather to interview him for a school assignment. One of the questions was what his vocation was and how he happened to choose it. This was his response:

"Vocation is not exactly what the questions suggest. It is God's plan for one's life. That plan is an entire life of good deeds he has prepared for one to 'walk in' (see Ephesians 2.10) — that is, to do. One finds out what that is by discerning, and one can do that only within the framework of all that one knows by faith.

"First, one can be sure that God does not want one to do anything bad, even if it is only a venial sin.

"Second, one finds oneself with various gifts — that is, capacities — that may need to be developed through education and practice. One can be sure that God meant one to use these gifts to do good things.

"Third, one sees that other people have various needs. Since everybody should be regarded as one's neighbor, one can be sure God wants one to do what one can to meet some of those needs.

"Fourth, God has made it clear that, for absolutely everybody, one need is more important than any other: to enter into the heavenly kingdom. Accepting the gospel, taking up one's cross, and following Jesus is the only sure way to do that. So, one knows that one should give priority to using one's gifts to meet others' need to hear and accept the gospel, to see the point of following Jesus, and to do that.

"Fifth, there are a lot of people, and all of them have a lot more needs than one can try to do anything about. So, one can be sure that God means one to consider all of one's gifts and also all of one's limitations, consider all the opportunities one sees for developing and using one's gifts in service to meet others' needs, consider which of those opportunities are more likely to help people hear and accept the gospel and follow Jesus, and then — all these things considered — to ask the Holy Spirit to help one identify what God wants one to try to do."

The man then went on to speak of his personal vocation and his granddaughter's.

Many things could be said about this compact presentation of vocational discernment. Here I make only this point: The question in this book's title — ministry or apostolate? — is not at its heart about programs and institutions and organizations (how to recruit and train people for this thing or that), nor is it about demographics and statistics (why are certain numbers going down — or up, for that matter — and what can be done about it?). These matters are important but not central.

Rather, the question is at its heart a question about the mysterious reality called vocation and it must be answered as such. People should organize their lives around their personal vocations. That the laity rarely are encouraged to do that is beside the point — except, of course, that it is a disastrous omission. The Church's duty is to hold up both things, apostolate and ministry, as realistic options for vocational choice, so that people can respond to a call to either or both once the call is heard.

The disproportionate emphasis on lay ministries in recent decades and the corresponding neglect of lay apostolate make it very difficult for that to happen. It is time for a change.

New Thinking

There are signs here and there that the change may have begun. Right along, Pope John Paul II has taken a sound view of these matters. It may be that the bishops of the United States are starting to do the same. Consider this from a 1998 bishops' statement called *Everyday Christianity*:

> Catholicism does not call us to abandon the world, but to help shape it. This does not mean leaving worldly tasks and responsibilities, but transforming them. Catholics are everywhere in this society. We are corporate executives and migrant farm workers, senators and welfare recipients, tradesmen and farmers, office and factory workers, union leaders and small business owners. Our entire community of faith must help Catholics be instruments of God's grace and creative power . . . in all the events of daily life.

Reading that, one feels like exclaiming, "*Now* you're talking, Your Excellencies!"

To anyone looking at the situation realistically, though, it must be clear that it will take a great deal of work to change established thinking and practice. As a result of the nearly exclusive attention to ministry in official circles in the United States for over thirty years, the "ministry" mindset is solidly entrenched in many key places — in national offices and organizations, in diocesan chanceries, in parishes and local

Church institutions. Not a few people have a vested interest in what in some ways resembles a ministry industry. All this cannot be changed overnight. Nor can dynamic, appealing approaches to lay apostolate soon be reconstituted on a large scale after decades of severe neglect.

Even so, quite a few things can and should be done, right now and simultaneously. The heart of it is a new, better idea of vocation — specifically, *personal* vocation.

The idea is this:

God calls every Catholic to participate in the mission of the Church. This is what Pope John Paul means, for example, when he says in a 1991 encyclical on missionary work that "missionary activity . . . is the task of all the Christian faithful." Most people will not spend time working in "the missions," but everyone should do what she or he can to foster and practice evangelization.

Confusion about the meaning of the word "vocation" and what it signifies drowns out the universal call to mission. That confusion is apparent when "vocation" is used to refer exclusively to callings to the clerical state and the religious life. Then it becomes easy to imagine that *only* the clergy and religious have vocations.

In reality, every Christian has a vocation. It would be good, in fact, if people thought of themselves not just as "having" vocations but as living in a rich, multidimensional vocational context.

One of these dimensions is the common Christian vocation that comes from baptism and confirmation. It is the universal call to love God and neighbor and to do one's part in the mission of the Church.

This universal vocation is specified by the choice of a state of life or Christian lifestyle — as a layperson, married or single, a priest or a religious. Discernment, in its technical sense, is needed to perceive the state of life to which one is called by God. This is a serious task, since each state in life inevitably involves a complex network of demanding relationships and duties, together with its own special ways of participating in the Church's mission.

Finally, people's roles in God's plan become concrete and individualized in their personal vocations. As the grandfather quoted above explained to his granddaughter, a personal vocation includes not only the universal vocation common to all and vocation in the sense of one's state in life but the unique talents and interests and aversions, strengths and weaknesses, roles and relationships in and through which each of us is meant to live the Christian vocation, carry out the duties of one's state in life, and make a unique contribution to the Church's mission.

A personal vocation is a *complete* life plan. It includes absolutely everything, even "small" things like hobbies and holidays. It even extends to accepting and dealing with afflictions and handicaps: weaknesses that give rise to temptations, sickness, loss of loved ones, unjust treatment by others, failure in good projects, unemployment, and so forth.

In general terms, this is the framework within which to think about apostolate and ministry as potential elements of one's personal vocation.

Pope John Paul speaks of personal vocation when, for example, he says (in *Christifideles Laici*) that "*all* . . . are laborers in the vineyard" and "*each* is called by name." But the press kit for the Jubilee Day for Lay Ministers produced by the bishops' conference gets it wrong in asserting that any true vocation involves being "willing to prepare for ministry." That is true of a calling to an *ecclesial ministry*, but it overlooks — indeed, it denies — the fact that laypeople who are not called to ecclesial ministry have real personal vocations of which a call to lay apostolate is certainly part.

Formation for Apostolate and Ministry

What would a program look like that seriously tried to prepare Catholic laypeople for their part in the Church's mission? Sections 58 to 63 of Pope John Paul's *Christifideles Laici* lay out the essentials. The pope does not present a detailed plan, something impossible to do in a document meant to apply to the Church in every place, from poor missionary countries to wealthy sophisticated places like the United States; but he does indicate some basic elements of lay formation that should be present everywhere.

The first of these revolves around what has just been discussed, that is, vocational discernment: "The fundamental objective of the formation of the lay faithful is an ever-clearer discovery of one's vocation and the ever-greater willingness to live it so as to fulfill one's mission." The pope makes it clear that he does not mean vocation in some general, generic sense (and certainly not in a narrow, clericalist one) but in the sense of *personal* vocation.

> God calls me and sends me forth as a laborer in his vineyard. He calls me and sends me forth to work for the coming of his Kingdom in history. This personal vocation and mission defines the dignity and responsibility of each member of the lay faithful and makes up the focal point of the whole work of formation.

So in forming people for lay apostolate and lay ministry, the starting point is to help them see what special thing God wants them to do.

For some, this will be a particular apostolate in a secular setting; for some, a ministry within the Church; for some, quite possibly both. Those who are responsible for the lay formation program should not prejudge the results of the discernment process, try to fit everyone into the same mold, or suppose that, once an individual has practiced vocational discernment, its results are set in concrete and discernment need never be done again. The discernment of one's personal vocation is a continuing process, a lifelong task: It is the effort to find God's will in the constantly changing circumstances of life. That is something that takes continuing prayer, study, reflection, and consultation with wise advisers.

John Henry Newman makes this point in a sermon on "Divine Calls."

> They who are living religiously, have from time to time truths they did not know before, or had no need to consider, brought before them forcibly; truths which involve duties, which are in fact precepts, and claim obedience. In this and such-like ways Christ calls us here and now. There is nothing miraculous or extraordinary in his dealings with us. . . . The accidents and events of life are, as is obvious, one special way in which the calls I speak of come to us.

That is to say the "accidents and events of life" are matter for vocational discernment; and, as such, they belong to formation.

Pope John Paul next makes another fundamental point: Formation should have as its aim bringing about what Vatican Council II called "unity of life." Laypeople must not think of themselves as living two separate lives, a "religious" life in church and a "secular" life in the world. "In fact," says the pope, "every area of the lay faithful's lives, as different as they are, enters into the plan of God."

> Every activity, every situation, every precise responsibility — as, for example, skill and solidarity in work, love and dedication in the family and the education of children, service to society and public life and the promotion of truth in the area of culture — are the occasions ordained by Providence for a "continuous exercise of faith, hope and charity."

He then lists various aspects of a "totally integrated formation" of laypeople in the context of unity of life. These aspects include both spiritual and doctrinal dimensions (with special attention to the Church's social doctrine), as well as "the cultivation of human values" (among other things, laypeople should learn to be good at what they do, since working well is part of their vocation and part of the apostolate).

Where and by whom is formation given? First of all, the pope says, people are formed by God; but beyond that, Catholics are formed by the Church. Within the Church, formation takes place in and through dioceses and parishes, as well as in small church communities, Christian families, Catholic schools and universities, and Catholic groups, associations, and movements, which provide formation through "a deeply shared experience in the apostolic life."

"Formation is not the privilege of a few, but a right and duty of all," John Paul declares at the close of this section of his important document. He adds that "the formation of those who will form others" calls for "appropriate courses or suitable schools"; forming the laity who will be responsible for forming others is "a basic requirement of assuring the general and widespread formation of all." One might add that forming the laity for apostolate and ministry is itself an important ministry, as suitable to properly formed laypeople as it is to priests. Preparing people for this work should be a major part of the degree- and certificate-granting programs for prospective full-time lay ecclesial ministers now springing up in many seminaries and Catholic schools.

Clearly, though, forming lay ministers to form other lay ministers should not be at the expense of forming people for lay apostolate, as currently is so often the case. In principle, the proliferation of ministry training programs is a good thing; but the neglect of formation for lay apostolate is not. A few apostolic groups and organizations, such as Opus Dei and the Legionaries of Christ, are doing effective work in this line, and a few centers and think tanks — for example, the National Center for the Laity, a liberally oriented Chicago spin-off of the 1977 Declaration of Christian Concern — push the idea. But only a small number of Catholic laypeople are reached. (The National Center for the Laity, P.O. Box 291102, Chicago, IL 60629, puts out a newsletter called *Initiatives* that regularly publishes relevant items about formation programs. Subscriptions are $15.00.)

'Social' and 'Ecclesial' — Friends or Foes?

Some interesting thinking on these matters has been done lately at the Newman Centre of McGill University in Montreal, source of *The Newman Rambler*, a twice-yearly journal that publishes some of the freshest and most creative ideas about the Catholic laity and lay apostolate currently to be found anywhere in North America. (Subscriptions for a minimum donation of $10.00, payable to The Newman Centre, are available from the Newman

Centre of McGill University, 3484 Peel Street, Montreal, Quebec, H3A 1W8 Canada.)

The Newman Centre's Daniel Cere notes two different types of lay groups visible in the Church: the "social" and the "ecclesial." Although it is common to think of them as being in conflict, he says, both have important contributions to make to serious reflection on the role of the laity and the question of lay formation.

Beginning with the social movements, Cere argues that in two ways the traditional approach to lay social action tended to overlook "the mainstream aspects of lay life in the world." First, lay activity was seen as "an effort to fill in the gaps created by the social system" rather than as having a significant influence upon the "normative institutions" that shape the lives of the laity (government, schools, media, business and the professions, etc.). Second, lay social action was defined as consisting almost exclusively of "those volunteer efforts which one can squeeze in between the more demanding commitments of work and family."

Lately, some groups have begun to resist this approach to lay life. By way of illustration, Cere cites efforts, often of non-Catholic Christian inspiration, originating among business people and attorneys (the "Religious Lawyering Movement"). "These lay movements are attempting to draw men and women together within their callings and to creatively explore the roots of their work in the light of their faith. They recognize that work constitutes a very significant component of one's life in terms of time and energy. They recognize that the failure to creatively link, connect, integrate a dimension that involves so much of our physical, intellectual, relational, and emotional life can entail a tragic fragmentation," he says.

Turning next to the ecclesial movements, Cere suggests that they are in healthy contrast with the "beige Christianity" preferred in most programs of education and formation for the laity since Vatican Council II; this nondescript religiosity "doesn't offend, doesn't stand out or contrast, it blends in with the general cultural milieu. . . . It is dull, uninteresting, and does not sell." But the new Catholic lay groups that emerged in the twentieth century — Catholic Action, Focolare, L'Arche, Communion and Liberation, the Charismatic Renewal, the Covenant Community Movement, Cursillo, the Neocate-chumenal Way, Regnum Christi, Opus Dei — reflect "a lay dynamism percolating within the internal life of the Church" and moving "out into the world." Such groups, he says, possess "a sharp sense of apostolic mission."

> Each movement seems to incarnate a specific charism — a specific form of evangelical outreach. They radiate outward, but they reach out in order to draw in, to draw the world, individual, culture into a deeper participation in the rich ecclesial reality of Christianity. [They] are animated by an evangelical spirit to bring the world to Christ.

Cere identifies six elements of such groups that he judges necessary for the lay vocation to survive and flourish: a foundational vision that relates the Christian tradition to contemporary life; a "transformative catechesis" embodied in programs of ongoing formation; emphasis on building and sustaining ecclesial communion in the face of the isolation that demoralizes many Christians in their aggressively secularized work and living environments; self-government and autonomy ("The institutional and organizational impoverishment of the laity undercuts their ability to engage in effective lay action"); the celebration of both marriage and celibacy in the face of a secular culture that denigrates both; and a commitment to venture and mission.

The temptation of the ecclesial groups, Cere suggests, is to become "too exclusively ecclesial" — too churchy and clericalist in their thinking, one might say; their strength is their rootedness in vocation and faith. The temptation of the social action groups is to lose sight of the need for "ongoing conversion and transformation"; their strength is to reject "the compartmentalization of work from faith." Each expression of lay mission and activism can learn a lot from the other.

Toward a New Catholic Subculture

Steps along the lines suggested here will be steps toward putting in place major elements of the new Catholic subculture that the Catholic community in the United States so badly needs as a basis, a grounding, for efforts to evangelize the secular culture. (These are efforts, one might add, that hardly exist today.)

Recall "St. Leo's Parish" in the pastoral letter on ministry by Los Angeles's Cardinal Mahony. It is described as a place where people understand that there can be no return to the days before the Second Vatican Council, "when there were large numbers of priests, sisters and brothers, and when the role of the laity in ministry seemed unnecessary and was inadequately recognized." The people of this mythical parish — and the cardinal who writes about them — are entirely correct: Those days are gone.

A parish of many ministers and many ministries has gone about half of the way required to respond to the new situation. But only half of the way.

A parish attempting realistically to respond to the full range of needs would also be a place where, in Cardinal Mahony's words, "one and all are challenged to exercise their baptismal calling." And not only challenged but formed. And formed not only to exercise the baptismal calling in cozy Church settings — to do ministry, in other words — but also consciously to take the risk of living out their baptismal calling in the complex and sometimes hostile environment of the secular world. In such a parish, people would be motivated (by continuing vocational discernment) and formed (by catechesis, liturgy, and prayer) to play their part in the Church's mission through lay ministry, certainly, but also through lay apostolate, carried on either individually or in collaboration with others.

But apostolate directed to what end? In his important document on the laity *Christifideles Laici* (cited here many times already), Pope John Paul identifies eight areas that call for the special attention of laypeople today: the dignity and rights of the person; respect for life; religious liberty; marriage and family; works of charity; politics and public life; social and economic justice; and the evangelization of culture through participation in academic life, scientific and technological research, and the arts, humanities, and media. There may be others, but these will do for a start.

If the Catholic laity of the United States — not alone, certainly, but working in cooperation with other persons of good will — were to tackle this agenda in a serious, intelligent manner, the Church would be well on its way to being the "culture-forming counterculture" of which George Weigel speaks. The extent to which that happens, he adds, will be "one of the great stories at the intersection of religion and American public life" during the twenty-first century.

There is, however, a real, and arguably unresolvable, tension between the vision of American Catholicism entertained by Weigel and others like him, and a different vision entertained by other Catholics, no less serious-minded and committed, who point out how decadent and destructive of faith American secular culture truly has become.

The priority for Catholics now, these people argue, is not evangelizing and converting this culture — which, humanly speaking, may be beyond redemption — but protecting themselves and their children against its virulent effects through a deliberate program of withdrawal into enclaves of orthodox faith and morality.

Marshall Fightlin, a Minnesota psychologist, suggests that certain secular professions and lines of work are today so corrupt that it is very nearly impossible for a faithful Catholic to take part in them without extraordinary precautions. Moreover, "as it becomes increasingly difficult to be a Catholic in the field of work, it will become imperative that we group together, not only to counter the ridicule and marginalization, but also to counter job loss."

Suggesting the organizing of "businesses, places of work, which are operated according to Catholic principles," he writes: "We are in desperate need, not only of truly Catholic (not necessarily parochial) schools, hospitals, health and mental health facilities, and universities, but also of truly Catholic law firms, drug companies, pharmacies, banks, insurance companies, and media. What is needed is nothing less than a well-ordered Catholic sub-culture."

In many respects, I believe, this is correct. But even supposing it is, it nonetheless remains within the realm of possibility that Catholics who are prudent and tenacious — and lucky — can achieve much good within secular structures and institutions. The danger of being corrupted in such settings is, of course, very great (but it also is present, and perhaps in more insidious ways, in some "Catholic" institutions that have lost their Catholic identity but continue to claim a relationship with the Church).

In any case, the building of the subculture is necessary. As that proceeds, the temptation sometimes will be strong to use it only as a refuge for a faithful remnant rather than a place of formation for apostolate. That temptation should be resisted; but it is imperative that American Catholics have a supportive cultural environment of faith in order to be, or become, a culture-forming counterculture.

The great mistake of the Catholic intellectuals who encouraged the dismantling of the old Catholic subculture in the 1950s and 1960s lay in overlooking an elementary fact: The Church needs an infrastructure of institutional supports and reinforcements of faith in order long to survive in the face of today's dominant, hostile secular culture. Unlike the Roman Empire in the days of the Epistle to Diognetus, this is a culture that has become adept at absorbing people through cultural assimilation. The pagan Romans persecuted Christians; today's neo-pagan secularists have discovered that it is more effective to co-opt them.

Cardinal Avery Dulles, S.J., makes both of these points. On the one hand, he says, "because the secular world is preponderantly antithetical to Christian revelation, faith requires for its growth an alternative environment, under the guidance of masters who are well grounded in Christian doctrine and exemplary in conduct." This is the Catholic subculture, or, as Joseph Varacalli calls it in the language of social science, the Catholic "plausibility structure." At the same time, as Cardinal Dulles also points out, the challenge for Catholics goes beyond simply creating an "alternative environment." The entire Church, he says, must commit itself to "the project of a new evangelization, new in ardor, methods, and expression."

It is not either/or. Both things are necessary.

A Spirituality for Ministry and Apostolate

Ruminating on the loss of the transmission belt for faith formerly supplied by the Catholic subculture, George Weigel suggests that "worship" now must get the job done. "*Lex orandi, lex credendi* [the law of prayer is the law of belief] is where this all starts and stops," he says. But even though the public worship of the Church is indeed essential to transmitting faith, it is not sufficient by itself; the institutions of a restored subculture also are indispensable. (Not necessarily all of the ambiguously "Catholic" institutions of the present day, however. One thinks, for example, of some Catholic periodicals and publishing houses, some Catholic schools and formation programs, which appear to be doing more to undermine faith than foster it. They are not only *not* indispensable but could and should be dispensed with.)

At the same time, for Catholic laypeople the starting point unquestionably must be an appropriate spirituality — a spirituality for apostolate *and* ministry. In conclusion, then, a few thoughts about that.

Pope John Paul quotes St. Francis de Sales on the subject of spirituality and the laity: "It is an error, or rather a heresy, to try to banish the devout life from the regiment of soldiers, the shop of the mechanic, the court of princes, or the home of married folk. It is true . . . that a purely contemplative, monastic, and religious devotion cannot be exercised in such ways of life. But besides these three kinds of devotion, there are several others adapted to bring to perfection those who live in the secular state."

The pope also quotes Vatican Council II: "This lay spirituality should take its particular character from the circumstances of one's state in life (married and family life, celibacy, widowhood), from one's state of health and from one's professional and social activity."

For laywomen and laymen, as for clerics and religious, at the heart of the fundamental option of faith is a personal relationship with God and a vibrant human relationship with Jesus Christ. Embracing a body of doctrines — the truths of God definitively revealed in and by Christ and taught by his Church — and striving to live the Christian life are inseparably part of it.

Faith is not private in any individualistic sense, however — "me and God." Faith necessarily has a communal dimension. Entering into a personal relationship with God our Father and Jesus our Savior, we enter also into a relationship with all God's children and all those Jesus came to save.

This is to say that in making the commitment of faith, we become members of a faith community, the Church, which nurtures and sustains us in the Christian life. And the implications of the faith we profess impel us to look beyond the community of faith, to the world at large — to see all men and women as our neighbors and seek ways to serve them in the manner of the Good Samaritan.

The Eucharist unites both dimensions of faith — personal relationship with the Lord, community with other people — in an extraordinary synthesis. These are twinned consequences of participating in the Eucharistic sacrifice and receiving the Body and Blood of Christ.

On the one hand, sharing the Eucharist has an irreducibly personal character. "The celebration of the Eucharistic sacrifice," the *Catechism of the Catholic Church* says, "is wholly directed toward the intimate union of the faithful with Christ" in his sacrificial act and in the communion with God to which it leads. But participation in the Eucharist also forms us into an outward-looking community, with a mission to love and serve our neighbors, above all those who are in material or spiritual need.

Evangelization is not a program by which Catholics try to gain control of the levers of secular power. It is service rendered to people who need to hear the good news of Christ, accept their redemption from sin and death, and experience the grace of God at work in their lives.

Individuals must learn for themselves, by vocational discernment, what specific form God wants this service to take for them. There are many excellent parish, diocesan, and community programs, many ministries, in which opportunities and unmet needs of all kinds can be found; and some people will undoubtedly conclude that they are called to work on their own, without joining any organized group.

In all cases Catholics are obliged to engage in apostolate — to give witness to the Gospel in word and deed, at home and in the neighborhood, at school, in the workplace, wherever they are. This is a duty arising from baptism and confirmation for which the Eucharist provides the vitality and reason.

What should the laity be doing — ministry or apostolate? The correct answer, as I said at the start, is: Both.

APPENDIX

Shared Responsibility

This book is not greatly concerned with issues of authority and governance. Whether the laity's role in the mission of the Church takes the form of lay ministry or lay apostolate, it should not be a quest for power. It would be tragic if it became one.

All the same, it is hardly possible to speak of the laity's role without at least touching on the question of shared responsibility — that is, on lay participation in the decision-making process in the Church.

Since Vatican Council II, parish and diocesan pastoral councils have been its major vehicles. There is not as much talk about pastoral councils these days as there was in the years just after Vatican II. Has the novelty worn off or is there some other reason? It is my impression that pastoral councils are established, effective structures in some places, rubber stamps for pastors and bishops elsewhere, and non-existent in still other locales. (A pastor — a very good one in many respects — once explained to me why he didn't have a pastoral council in his parish and had no intention of having one: "If I want advice, I ask somebody. I don't need a council for that." How widespread is that attitude?)

Maybe the time has come for a fresh look at pastoral councils. In particular, it may be time to dust off the idea of a National Pastoral Council for the Catholic Church in the United States, which for all practical purposes was scuttled a quarter of a century ago.

Two events in 2001 were reminders that creating some such body as a National Pastoral Council really is part of the unfinished post-Vatican II business of the Church in the United States. In mid-summer, the National Conference of Catholic Bishops (NCCB) and the United States Catholic Conference (USCC) ceased to exist, and a new entity called the United States Conference of Catholic Bishops (USCCB) took their place. October brought the twenty-fifth anniversary of the once-famous Call To Action Conference in Detroit. The scheme for a National Pastoral Council is tied up with all of these things.

Some history makes it clear why that is so.

Ecclesiastical Alphabet Soup:
NCWC to NCCB/USCC to USCCB

From World War I until the mid-1960s, American bishops sponsored an agency called the National Catholic Welfare Conference to coordinate their voluntary cooperation at the national level. It was replaced in 1966, immediately after Vatican II, by NCCB and USCC. An unusual feature of the new institution was its dual-conference structure: NCCB was the episcopal conference, mandated by the recent Council, through which the bishops were to collaborate with one another in carrying out the pastoral agenda it had set for them; as for USCC, it often was said that it was intended to represent the social action interests of the bishops. This was true up to a point, but there was more to it than that.

USCC was indeed NCCB's "social action" twin, with

departments responsible for education, communications, and what in time came to be called social development and world peace. But its creators also envisaged it as the nucleus from which in time a National Pastoral Council would evolve, embodying the "shared responsibility" for the Church celebrated during and after Vatican II. The fundamental idea of shared responsibility was that priests, deacons, religious, and laypeople would collaborate with the bishops in specified areas of decision making. In the United States Cardinal John Dearden of Detroit, first president of NCCB/USCC, was a leading proponent of this idea.

As a step in the direction of shared responsibility, non-bishops served along with bishops as voting members of the policy-formulating committees of the three USCC departments. This was in contrast with the NCCB committees, where only bishops served as members and had the vote. Another, potentially even more important step was taken in 1969 with the establishment of a National Advisory Council, composed of bishops and non-bishops, to exercise oversight over USCC and its civic-political agenda. "A functioning Advisory Council was seen as a hoped-for instance of shared responsibility in the Church at the national level," Cardinal Dearden wrote in 1975.

One of this Advisory Council's first projects was to study the feasibility of a National Pastoral Council. The study culminated in a conference held at Mundelein College, Chicago, in August, 1970, with one hundred one dioceses and thirty-six national organizations represented. The Advisory Council reported to the bishops the following year that a National Pastoral Council was desirable but not immediately possible — more spadework was needed before going ahead.

In January of 1973, however, the Vatican's Congregation for the Clergy sent the world's bishops a letter saying National Pastoral Councils were not opportune. The letter was apparently occasioned by the performance of the Dutch Pastoral Council in controversial events then unfolding in The Netherlands under the rubric of "renewal." Very likely the letter also was a response to the feasibility study in the United States.

'Call To Action'

Although the Vatican had spoken, the NPC idea was not dead. The Advisory Council had suggested that such a body be up and running by the time of the U.S. Bicentennial in 1976. The bishops in 1973 established a Bicentennial committee under Cardinal Dearden to plan the Church's official participation in the national celebration. The centerpiece of the program turned out to be the Call To Action conference. In retrospect, it appears to have been an effort to reintroduce the NPC concept by the back door. Instead, it had the opposite result.

A majority of the thirteen hundred delegates who gathered that October 21-23 in Detroit were employed by Church agencies. In his memoirs, conservative writer Russell Kirk, who was there, mischievously called these people "church mice." But if the description is accurate, these were church mice feeling their oats. In resolutions that ranged from birth control to the arms race, they advocated women's ordination, married priests, admission of divorced and remarried Catholics to the sacraments, a national arbitration board with the power to undo bishops' decisions, and a great deal else corresponding to secular and religious ideas of political correctness at that time.

Holy Cross College historian David O'Brien, one of the planners of the bishops' Bicentennial program, writes: "The democratic process, which saw a lay person having the same vote as a bishop, and the progressive nature of the resolutions made many members of the hierarchy nervous, so that its results were more or less shelved." Along with the idea of a National Pastoral Council.

Even so, the institutional germ of the NPC scheme continued to exist in the form of the United States Catholic Conference, with its mixed-membership committees, and in the behind-the-scenes activities of the National Advisory Council. As of mid-summer of 2001, much of that changed.

The reorganization plan for the American bishops' conference that then went into effect had been developed through a process initially headed by the late Cardinal Joseph Bernardin of Chicago and continued under Archbishop Daniel Pilarczyk of Cincinnati. (Both had been presidents of NCCB/USCC.) Scrapping the old dual-conference structure, the plan replaced it with a unitary entity, the United States Conference of Catholic Bishops, as the episcopal conference of the United States. Program and staff (laity, religious, clergy) looked very much as in the past; the National Advisory Council remained. But, in accord with canon law governing episcopal conferences, the new USCCB restricts voting membership on its committees to bishops, with non-bishops serving as consultants only.

This change is hardly likely to have much visible impact on Catholic life. But even so it marks a further move away from the postconciliar vision of shared responsibility. That in itself is a reason to revisit the idea of a National Pastoral Council now.

There are other reasons as well.

The Case for a National Pastoral Council

One reason lies in the fact that the Catholic community in the United States has civic and political effectiveness far short of what its size would suggest. About one American in every four is a Catholic, yet on issues from abortion to capital punishment, from educational vouchers to marriage and family, this body of some sixty-three million people does not have an impact on public policy that might be expected, considering its numbers.

There are many reasons for that. Some, though hardly all, have been examined in this book. Prominent among them are the abandonment of the ideal of lay apostolate, whether as Catholic Action or in any other form, the collapse of the old Catholic subculture, and the unmediated assimilation of large numbers of Catholics into a secular culture indifferent or hostile to Catholic values.

Another source of the problem is the lack of an effective national structure through which lay Catholics can participate in formulating and representing the Church's views on public policy. As matters stand, on many political issues the bishops resemble generals without troops. The United States Conference of Catholic Bishops, as a "pure" bishops' organization, will hardly change this situation for the better.

Other good purposes might also be served by establishing a National Pastoral Council. For example, it could help Catholics move beyond time-wasting and sterile debates about the seamless garment and the common ground, by participating together in purposeful dialogue concerning real policy issues. It might also give a boost to ecumenical relations, especially with the Orthodox and the Anglicans, by serving as a practical step in the direction of a synodal process for decision making.

If earlier mistakes are to be avoided, much consultation, discussion, and careful planning should precede the creation of any such body. The concerns of the Holy See and the implications for the Church elsewhere should be respected. It would be important to weigh the meaning of the fact that the Code of Canon Law provides for *diocesan* pastoral councils but is silent about national counterparts. Among the matters needing particularly close attention are these:

- The makeup of a National Pastoral Council. It should not be overloaded with middle-echelon Church bureaucrats, as happened at the Call To Action conference. Clear norms would be required regarding things like categories of membership and method of selection. Non-bishop members should represent the spectrum of legitimate opinion in the Church, without overloading in the direction of political, economic, and social liberalism or conservatism; they should include a good number who fully understand and accept Catholic social teaching, which often runs contrary to the agendas of both the secular left and the secular right.

- The agenda of a National Pastoral Council. Should it be limited to public policy or should it also consider questions pertaining to the internal life of the Church? At the very least, a go-slow approach would be in order, lest the National Pastoral Council repeat Call To Action's mistake of speaking too quickly and too simplistically about too much.

- The weight carried by decisions of a National Pastoral Council. In *Novo Millennio Ineunte*, his apostolic letter for the close of Jubilee Year 2000, Pope John

Paul mentioned pastoral councils — presumably diocesan — among the "structures of participation" that ought to be encouraged for the sake of ecclesial communion. He said such bodies are "consultative rather than deliberative," but no less "meaningful and relevant" on that account. The hope would be that through the National Pastoral Council the bishops over time would provide for, oversee, and support the development of an authentically lay apostolate in the political, social, and economic realms at the national level.

Thought also should be given to the possibility of eventually creating a local-state-national network of pastoral councils. The National Pastoral Council would be a more significant and effective body if it had links to the grassroots.

This is a lot to talk about. The conversation should begin. When it does, it should be in the spirit of *Novo Millennio Ineunte*, which strongly commends "the ancient pastoral wisdom which, without prejudice to their authority, encouraged Pastors to listen more widely to the entire People of God."

ABOUT THE AUTHOR

Russell Shaw, a former Secretary for Public Affairs of the National Conference of Catholic Bishops, is a consultor to the Pontifical Council for Social Communications, having been appointed to that office by Pope John Paul II.

He is the author or coauthor of more than a dozen books, including *Our Sunday Visitor's Encyclopedia of Catholic Doctrine* and *Papal Primacy in the Third Millennium*. He is also the editor of *The Pope Speaks*, a publication of Our Sunday Visitor, as well as *Our Sunday Visitor* newspaper's Washington correspondent. In addition, he is a *Columbia* magazine contributing editor.

Among other publications in which his work has appeared are *Crisis*, *Lay Witness*, *The Newman Rambler*, and *Palabra* (Madrid).

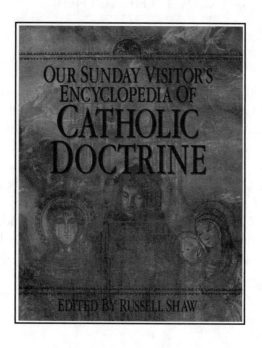

Everything you've ever wanted to know about
Catholic dogma in one convenient volume.
0-87973-746-8 (746), hardcover, 728 pp.
0-87973-774-3 (774), CD-ROM

To order from Our Sunday Visitor:
Toll free: 1-800-348-2440
E-mail: osvbooks@osv.com
Website: www.osv.com

Availability of products subject to change without notice.

An in-depth look at the attempts to "tame" the papacy
from a historical perspective and a theological view.
0-87973-555-4 (555), paper, 192 pp.

To order from Our Sunday Visitor:
Toll free: 1-800-348-2440
E-mail: osvbooks@osv.com
Website: www.osv.com

Availability of products subject to change without notice.

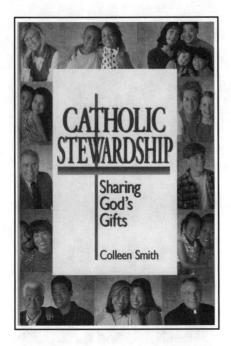

What does Jesus ask of us? Catholic stewardship! Imagine what would happen if Catholics everywhere shared the gifts of time, ability, and treasure they have been entrusted with. Designed with you in mind, this booklet will motivate you to take the first steps, bringing joy and goodness to yourself and others.

0-9707756-4-4 (Inventory No. T1), paper, 80 pp.

To order from Our Sunday Visitor:
Toll free: 1-800-348-2440
E-mail: osvbooks@osv.com
Website: www.osv.com

Availability of products subject to change without notice.

Our Sunday Visitor. . .
*Your Source for Discovering
the Riches of the Catholic Faith*

Our Sunday Visitor has an extensive line of materials for young children, teens, and adults. Our books, Bibles, booklets, CD-ROMs, audios, and videos are available in bookstores worldwide.

To receive a FREE full-line catalog or for more information, call **Our Sunday Visitor** at **1-800-348-2440**. Or write, **Our Sunday Visitor** / 200 Noll Plaza / Huntington, IN 46750.

- -

Please send me: ___A catalog
Please send me materials on:
___Apologetics and catechetics   ___Reference works
___Prayer books   ___Heritage and the saints
___The family   ___The parish
Name_____
Address_____
City_____Apt._____
_____State_____Zip_____
Telephone (   ) _____

A23BBABP

- -

Please send a friend: ___A catalog
Please send a friend materials on:
___Apologetics and catechetics   ___Reference works
___Prayer books   ___Heritage and the saints
___The family   ___The parish
Name_____
Address_____
City_____Apt.____
_____State_____Zip_____
Telephone (   ) _____

A23BBA

- -

Our Sunday Visitor
200 Noll Plaza
Huntington, IN 46750
Toll free: 1-800-348-24
E-mail: osvbooks@osv
Website: www.osv.com

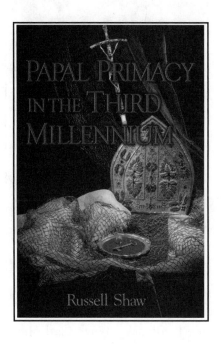

An in-depth look at the attempts to "tame" the papacy
from a historical perspective and a theological view.
0-87973-555-4 (555), paper, 192 pp.

To order from Our Sunday Visitor:
Toll free: 1-800-348-2440
E-mail: osvbooks@osv.com
Website: www.osv.com

Availability of products subject to change without notice.

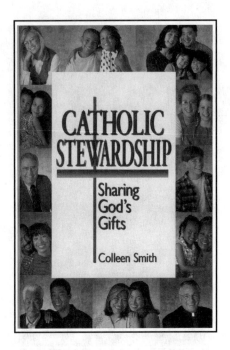

What does Jesus ask of us? Catholic stewardship! Imagine what would happen if Catholics everywhere shared the gifts of time, ability, and treasure they have been entrusted with. Designed with you in mind, this booklet will motivate you to take the first steps, bringing joy and goodness to yourself and others.

0-9707756-4-4 (Inventory No. T1), paper, 80 pp.

To order from Our Sunday Visitor:
Toll free: 1-800-348-2440
E-mail: osvbooks@osv.com
Website: www.osv.com

Availability of products subject to change without notice.

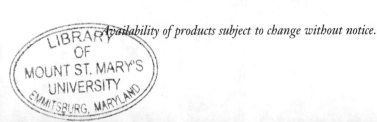

Our Sunday Visitor. . .
Your Source for Discovering the Riches of the Catholic Faith

Our Sunday Visitor has an extensive line of materials for young children, teens, and adults. Our books, Bibles, booklets, CD-ROMs, audios, and videos are available in bookstores worldwide.

To receive a FREE full-line catalog or for more information, call **Our Sunday Visitor** at **1-800-348-2440**. Or write, **Our Sunday Visitor** / 200 Noll Plaza / Huntington, IN 46750.

- -

Please send me: ___A catalog
Please send me materials on:
___Apologetics and catechetics   ___Reference works
___Prayer books   ___Heritage and the saints
___The family   ___The parish
Name_____
Address_____Apt._____
City_____State_____Zip_____
Telephone (   ) _____

A23BBABP

- -

Please send a friend: ___A catalog
Please send a friend materials on:
___Apologetics and catechetics   ___Reference works
___Prayer books   ___Heritage and the saints
___The family   ___The parish
Name_____
Address_____Apt._____.
City_____State_____Zip_____
Telephone (   ) _____

A23BBABP

- -

Our Sunday Visitor
200 Noll Plaza
Huntington, IN 46750
Toll free: 1-800-348-2440
E-mail: osvbooks@osv.com
Website: www.osv.com